Organize Your
Garage
....In No Time

Barry Izsak

800 East 96th Street,
Indianapolis, Indiana 46290

Organize Your Garage In No Time

International Standard Book Number: 0-7897-3219-X

Library of Congress Catalog Card Number: 2004114915

Printed in the United States of America

First Printing: March 2005

08   07   06   05   4   3   2

Trademarks

Warning and Disclaimer

Bulk Sales

Que Publishing offers excellent discounts on this book when ordered in quantity for bulk purchases or special sales. For more information, please contact

U.S. Corporate and Government Sales
1-800-382-3419
corpsales@pearsontechgroup.com

For sales outside of the U.S., please contact

International Sales
international@pearsoned.com

Executive Editor
Candace Hall

Development Editor
Lorna Gentry

Managing Editor
Charlotte Clapp

Senior Project Editor
Matthew Purcell

Copy Editor
Bart Reed

Indexer
Erika Millen

Proofreader
Tonya Simpson

Technical Editor
Bill West, Paragon Garage Company, Ltd.

Publishing Coordinator
Cindy Teeters

Interior Designer
Anne Jones

Cover Designer
Anne Jones

Cover Illustrator
Nathan Clement, Stickman Studio

Page Layout
Eric S. Miller

Contents at a Glance

Table of Contents

About the Author

Barry Izsak, owner of ARRANGING IT ALL™ in Austin, Texas, has been helping corporate and residential clients nationwide get organized since 1996. He is a member of the National Association of Professional Organizers (NAPO), currently serving as president on its board of directors. Barry is a member of the NAPO Golden Circle, recipient of the 2002 NAPO President's Award, and an authorized consultant for Kiplinger's Taming the Paper Tiger® software. As an industry leader, Barry is in high demand as a speaker and trainer for organizations and major corporations nationwide. He is well known for his steadfast commitment to promoting the professional organizing industry. Major newspapers and magazines often quote Barry as an authoritative voice on home and office organization trends and news, and he has been featured on CNN and CNBC. For more information, visit www.ArrangingItAll.com.

Dedication

In memory of my loving parents,

Vickie and Manny Izsak,

whose influence

helped lay the foundation

for me to find my path

as a professional organizer.

Acknowledgments

To say that writing this book was a bigger task than I had anticipated would be an understatement. Without the unwavering support and assistance of so many, it would have been an even greater one. Their faith and belief in me made all the difference.

My sincerest and heartfelt thanks to the following:

Dan Slutsky, for his unconditional support and encouragement, as well as his photographic expertise and the countless hours he spent enhancing many of the photos in this book.

Valentina Sgro and Debbie Stanley, who each played a huge role in motivating me to continue writing and whose friendships I will always cherish.

Candace Hall, Lorna Gentry, Matt Purcell, Bart Reed, and the rest of the Que team for their steadfast patience, encouragement, and guidance throughout the writing process.

Bill West, for his technical expertise and assistance with this project.

All my friends and esteemed colleagues in NAPO who inspire me to be the best I can be and make me proud to represent this industry.

The many neighbors, friends, and total strangers with open garage doors who graciously allowed me to snap pictures inside their garages.

We Want to Hear from You!

As the reader of this book, *you* are our most important critic and commentator. We value your opinion and want to know what we're doing right, what we could do better, what areas you'd like to see us publish in, and any other words of wisdom you're willing to pass our way.

As an executive editor for Que Publishing, I welcome your comments. You can email or write me directly to let me know what you did or didn't like about this book—as well as what we can do to make our books better.

Please note that I cannot help you with technical problems related to the topic of this book. We do have a User Services group, however, where I will forward specific technical questions related to the book.

When you write, please be sure to include this book's title and author as well as your name, email address, and phone number. I will carefully review your comments and share them with the author and editors who worked on the book.

Email: feedback@quepublishing.com

Mail: Candace Hall
Executive Editor
Que Publishing
800 East 96th Street
Indianapolis, IN 46240 USA

For more information about this book or another Que Publishing title, visit our website at www.quepublishing.com. Type the ISBN (excluding hyphens) or the title of a book in the Search field to find the page you're looking for.

Preface

Evolution of the Garage

With the introduction of the first "horseless carriage," or motor car, in the late nineteenth century, America's love affair with the automobile began. With the introduction of the Model T in the early twentieth century, motor cars were passionately embraced by the American public. No longer a "toy for the rich," automobiles quickly worked their way into the mainstream middle class and became an essential item. By 1920, there were already more than nine million of them.

The logical next question everyone began asking was, "Where are we going to store them?"

Early cars were very expensive, and people wanted to protect their investment, so they stored them in old carriage houses and barns alongside the horses or in public livery stables. The latter option was the predecessor to today's public garage. For $15–$20 per month, a car could be stored there, and additional services were offered that would later be provided by full-service gas stations.

This arrangement proved to be very inconvenient and lasted only a short time, as people began to demand convenience and didn't want their cars to smell like horse manure. People questioned why they couldn't just store their cars at home. The big fear back then was the real danger that this motorized carriage could spontaneously burst into flames. The concept of attaching a garage to the house was unthinkable, so people began building free-standing wooden or brick structures to house their prized investment. From the French word *garer*, meaning "to protect," the concept of the garage as we know it today was born.

The early garages came in two varieties. They were either built in the same style as the main house, using leftover building materials, or were delivered as a kit from Sears or Montgomery Ward. The garages that came in these kits were more utilitarian and con-

The earliest garages were wooden structures detached from the main house.

structed of wood or metal. They were practical, affordable, and quick and easy to build. The use of windows was strictly for ventilation or light and not for architectural significance or interest.

Early garage doors were much more like barn doors. The weight and awkwardness of these unwieldy doors made them very impractical, especially for those who lived in snowy climates. Sliding doors were introduced next, but the garage needed to be wider in order for this type of door to work, and city dwellers did not have that kind of space. These were soon followed by the lift-type door, and though definitely an improvement, they were heavy and cumbersome.

These metal lift-type doors were lighter and easier to open than wooden doors.

In 1921, C.G. Johnson invented the overhead door. Although a definite improvement, it too was heavy for some people to lift. This problem was solved with the invention of the first automated garage door opener in 1926. Consumers loved this invention, but unfortunately few could afford it. This changed when the mass production of garage door openers began in the mid 1950s. However, it would be another 20 years before the use of these devices became widespread and affordable for the masses.

Early carports were usually made of wood, and some were very distinctive.

The carport was another option for protecting the car. It gained increasing popularity in the 1940s and is still widely used today. Especially popular in places with

warmer and more temperate climates such as Florida and California, carports were liked by builders because they were much less expensive to build than the traditional garage. Carports come in one- and two-car varieties and are usually constructed with a large closet-like enclosure to store tools, lawn and garden supplies, and the traditional items one would store in a garage. The storage space in a carport is much

Carports are still used today and help reduce building costs.

more limited, and good organization is critical for maximizing its use. A large number of the attached one-car garages seen today started out as carports that were later enclosed.

Attached garages became popular as a matter of convenience.

Not everyone embraced the concept of the attached garage right away. Many were not in favor of attached garages and resisted incorporating them as a part of their houses because they were viewed as unattractive. By the early 1940s, convenience prevailed and the attached garage became more common. Even the famous architect Frank Lloyd Wright incorporated one of the early attached garages into his Oak Park, Illinois home. However, it was not until the late 1950s that the attached garage became prevalent. Still, approximately half of American homes had a garage of some sort or a carport.

With the inner-city flight to the suburbs and increasing American affluence, it was clear that one car would no longer meet the needs of the suburban family. Two-car families became the norm, and by the end of the 1980s, the majority of homes being built had two-car garages.

Realtors claim that the garage is the amenity most requested by today's home-buyers and, as such, ranks above a large kitchen, formal dining room, and large backyard. In the last decade, even apart-ment dwellers have demanded the conven-ience of a garage, and builders are accommodating them.

Two-and-a-half-, three-, and even four-car garages are commonly featured in higher-priced homes. And as everything old becomes new again, builders are returning to the carriage house garage style of years ago, offering that as an option in newer residential communities.

Each side of this two-car garage has its own door.

Windows are a popular feature in doors for two-car garages.

Three- and four-car garages are becoming increasingly popular with today's homeowners.

Many apartment complexes now offer garages as an amenity.

Introduction

Introduction

When people discover that I am a professional organizer, many are quick to tell me that their homes are very organized—except for the garage! The one question that gets the biggest laugh whenever I ask it at the organizing workshops I lead is, "How many of you can park the number of cars in your garage it was designed to hold?" Unfortunately, it is also one of the questions for which very few hands go up. The bottom line is that most garages are so crammed with clutter that cars lose out. No one room of the house is a greater source of embarrassment or the butt of more jokes than the garage.

As you read in the preface to this book, "Evolution of the Garage," the trend in the building industry today is to build a bigger garage. The two-car garage has become the standard, and homeowners are now insisting on three- and four-car garages. Yet, I think most of us would agree that this does not mean the space is being utilized any better.

"Our home is our castle," as the old saying goes, and homeowners spend billions each year to make them just that. However, the one area of our homes where the door is open daily for the entire world to see also tends to be the most unsightly, poorly utilized, and neglected.

Why live with a garage that looks like this...

...when you can drive into a well-organized garage like this?

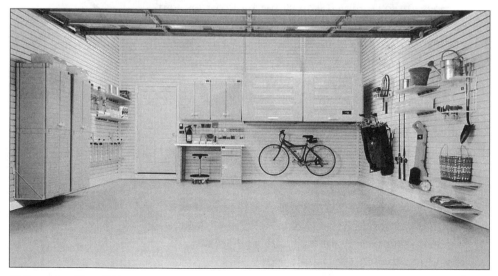

(Photo courtesy of GarageTek.)

Here is another saying: "Our stuff will grow to fill the space allotted." This could not be any truer than when it comes to the garage. Most of us don't know how or why it happened, and we certainly did not plan it intentionally, but the fact remains that when we can't find a place to put something, it ends up in the garage. That's why we need *Organize Your Garage In No Time.*

Who This Book Is Written For

This book is for you if you are embarrassed to open your garage door because the neighbors will see how you live. It's also written to help anyone who's tired of looking at all the clutter in the garage and wants to use it for the purpose for which it was designed—to park cars! Whether you are a man who wants the garage you have always fantasized about, a woman who is ready to tackle this job but not quite sure where to begin, or a child who wants to help with a major garage-cleaning project to earn some extra money, this book is for you.

You don't need to be a handyman or possess any special skills other than a desire to transform your garage from a dumping ground into an organized, integral part of your home. Although the garage has long been considered "the man's domain," this is certainly no longer the case. Everyone has a stake in making the garage more user friendly, and this book will help you do just that.

Here are some basic questions you need to ask yourself if you are truly committed to winning the war on clutter in your garage:

- Do I really need three lawnmowers (one of which doesn't work), two edge trimmers, five brooms, 46 flower pots, nine hammers, 27 screwdrivers, and two sets of socket wrenches (with a few attachments you aren't even sure how or why to use)?
- What good is it doing me to have so much stuff yet not be able to find it when I really need it or even remember that I have it?
- Is the top of my workbench so cluttered that I have no place to work on it?
- Does it make sense to park my expensive cars in the driveway or on the street because my garage is full of a bunch of stuff far less valuable that "I might need someday"?

And, before you think about selling your home to upgrade from a two-car garage to one that holds four, ask yourself one more question:

- Would my current garage would work just fine if it were organized and I had only what I needed and got rid of everything I hadn't used in the last year or two?

If these questions make you shudder as you face the organizational problems ahead, then this book is for you. *Organize Your Garage In No Time* can help you solve those problems and reclaim the garage for its intended use.

However, this book is not for everyone. If you are happy with a cluttered garage, don't really care if you ever park a car in it, don't want to know what stuff is buried out there, and don't mind that you are wasting space, then don't waste your time reading this book. Buy it for the other people you live with who are pushing you to get this job done or give it to a friend. But if you have had enough and really do want to use your garage for the purpose which it was intended, read on.

How This Book Will Help You

So, what's holding you back? What makes organizing the garage such a distasteful and intimidating task and one you tend to avoid at all costs? You want to do it and are even committed to doing it, but you keep putting it off and postponing the inevitable. Is it the quantity of stuff out there or the fact that you don't have enough time? Is it the fear that you won't do it right, or possibly a combination of all of these?

One of the biggest reasons people put this project off is that they are overwhelmed and simply don't know where to start. This reaction is very understandable. Let me illustrate. How many times have you chosen a Saturday and decided that this was the day you were going to clean out the garage? (OK, maybe you didn't exactly decide this on your own. Perhaps you were coerced by your significant other to do it, but that doesn't matter.)

So, you go out there with the best of intentions. The first item that catches your eye is an old lamp shade. You pick it up, ponder for a moment, and then you set it down two feet away because you aren't sure what to do with it. Next, you pick up an old bicycle tire and wonder if you still even have the bicycle it belongs to. You aren't really sure, so you put it aside, too. You pick up an old can of paint and shake it, but hear nothing. You know that you aren't supposed to dispose of it with the regular garbage, but you really don't know the proper way, so you set it aside as well. You spy the old weed eater you were going to have repaired; but in the meantime, your wife bought a new one for you last Father's Day. Before you know it, you are overcome with the decisions and choices you need to make and panic sets in. You convince yourself that this wasn't such a good idea after all and begin to wonder if the best decision of all is to put this project off for another day!

You want to organize your garage and you need help doing it. *Organize Your Garage In No Time* was written to help you do just that. It will enable you to tackle this project once and for all in the simplest, fastest, and most efficient way possible so you can spend your time doing the things you really enjoy. You have already taken the first step by buying this book. It will demystify and guide you through the process, step by step. In fact, it will make this project so painless you might actually enjoy doing it as much as you enjoy the final result!

Other self-help books of this type can be heavy on the theory and light on guiding the reader through the process. This book is the opposite. *Organize Your Garage In No Time* is the only partner you need to tackle the job. It starts out with some of the basics, but the bulk of the book is devoted to taking you through the project one step at a time. Of course, if you can enlist the help of family members or elect to hire a professional organizer to assist you, you can get the job done even faster. But remember, getting that assistance is purely optional; you can do this on your own!

After reading this book, you will learn how to do the following:

- Apply the basic organizing principles and steps of the organizing process to your garage-organizing project.
- Store items properly and maximize your use of space.
- Create and organize storage centers for specific items throughout the garage.
- Decide what to keep and what to get rid of.
- Properly dispose of the things you don't want.
- Conduct a successful garage sale if you decide to have one.

How to Use This Book

This book is organized into a series of parts, each containing chapters grouped into logical blocks of information. You'll also find a number of lists, icons, and special text elements to help make your reading more interesting and informative. The following sections explain more about the book's organization and elements, so you'll understand how to get the most from reading it.

How the Book Is Organized

Each of the book's parts contains specific types of information; as a result, you'll use each part differently. Here's what you'll find in *Organize Your Garage In No Time*:

- In Part I, "Garage Organizing Basics," you will learn the basic principles and rules of organizing and how to apply them to any portion of your garage-organizing project. Reading through the first part of the book will assist you in determining your objective and defining the scope of this project. You will learn the various and most appropriate ways to store items, as well as how to determine the type of storage solution that is right for you. If you already have a shelving or hanging storage solution you like, you can skip this section. However, my advice to you is that if you have the time, read it anyway because you just might be convinced to upgrade or change the system you are currently using.

- Next, turn to the specific chapter topic you need help with in Part II, "Creating Storage Centers: Everything Needs a Home," and begin your organizing project. Everything might not apply to you. You might not have any sporting goods but instead have lots of seasonal storage. By reading the relevant sections of this part of the book, you will pick up a lot of ideas to help you organize other portions of your home as well. With a small amount of determination, coupled with the practical suggestions and step-by-step guidance in this book, your garage will quickly become a source of pride for you and your family.

- Part III, "Beyond the Basics," is devoted to subjects that you will want to consider as your garage-organizing project nears completion. These will help answer any remaining questions you might have, including these:

Should I seal the garage floor?

What is the best way to get rid of things I no longer want?

Should I have a garage sale?

Using the Book's Special Elements

You will see a series of special text elements, icons, and lists throughout this book that identify key points and make your job easier. In addition to the traditional Notes, Tips, and Cautions, this book contains a number of sidebars, filled with useful and interesting information to supplement the book's coverage of the current task. To-Do Lists itemize the tasks you'll accomplish in each major section of the chapter, and Shopping Lists give you a quick check of all the tools, equipment, and supplies you'll need to get the job done.

In addition to these elements, you'll notice a number of graphical icons in the margin beside certain paragraphs of text. These icons are unique to this book and are used to mark specific types of information:

The Dollar Wise icon indicates an idea that can save you money.

The Safety icon is used to mark text that presents ideas intended to promote your personal safety—and that of your family.

The Take It to the Max icon indicates a high-end idea or product that will make your garage the envy of the neighborhood.

Barry's Best icons mark unique, simple, or easy ways to solve common problems.

Remember what I said earlier: You can do this. Whether you desire to have the garage of your dreams or simply to be able to find what you want, when you need it, your goal is achievable. It will take time and a commitment on your part, but if it is something you really want, this book will make it doable.

So, turn the page and let's get started!

Part I

Garage Organizing Basics

Where Do I Begin?

1

S o, you're all psyched up and ready to dive into your garage organization project. You have been putting this off for years, and your marital bliss or sanity could be at stake if you don't get moving. The clutter has reached the point of filling virtually every square inch of your garage, and you can barely get in and out of your car—that is, if your car still fits. Forget about trying to find anything in there. You gave up on that years ago.

If there is any hope of you ever being able to comfortably park a car in your garage—although at this point you would just be happy to see the floor again—you must be committed to doing everything possible to ensure your success and make this happen. Buying this book was a step in the right direction, and you have made up your mind that this time is going to be different!

Hold on a minute. What makes you so sure of that? Have you ever asked yourself why your prior attempts to do this were unsuccessful? What has changed that makes you think you will be successful this time? After all, it is the same garage and, if anything, the volume of clutter has increased.

Well, for one, I have given you my promise that I am going to guide you through the process step by step. You have my word on that. But even with that assurance, there are some things you need to think about before you dive into this project to ensure that the outcome will be the one you are looking for. I know you are anxious to get started, but just trust me on this. You need to think about how you want to use your garage and how you want it to look when you are finished with this project. In simplest terms, you need a plan. It doesn't have to be a complex one at all, but you need a clear vision so you will know when you have achieved success.

In this chapter you learn how to decide what you want your garage to be and how to create a plan that will help you reach that goal. From envisioning the final product to creating a step-by-step process for achieving it, this chapter walks you through this first important stage of your organization project. Along the way, you also learn a few basic tips for making sure you're storing items safely in your garage. And, before you shift a thing, read this chapter's quick guide to safe lifting.

To do list

- ☐ Analyze how you've been using your garage.
- ☐ Determine whether you need or want to use it differently.
- ☐ Assess your garage's "weatherability."

Analyzing Your Needs

Before you can analyze how you want to use your garage in the future, you need to consider how you have been using it up until now. Here are some points to consider:

- Has your garage been used to park cars?
- Do you have a functional workbench area? Is it large enough?
- How many bicycles and other types of large sporting equipment do you store in there?
- Do you store a lot of lawn and garden equipment, lawnmowers, a snow blower, and patio furniture in the off season?
- Are you using your wall and ceiling space effectively?
- Are you storing a lot of large and bulky items that are making your garage less functional and roomy?
- Has your garage become a disorganized maze of boxes and garbage bags and you have no clue what is inside any of them?

Are You Storing from Necessity or from Habit?

If you have not been using your garage to park your cars, then you need to ask yourself why. Is it because you don't want to or because there is no room? If your garage has begun to look like a disorganized storage facility, is this because you have not taken the time to sort through all the stuff and are putting off making a decision? Or is it that you really want and need all of this and just don't have enough place to store it or are not storing it efficiently? Or is it that up until now, you weren't motivated to do anything about it? The answers to all these questions will be very important in formulating your new plan and keeping your vision realistic.

Weathering the Elements

Not all garages are created equally. Some of them are more climate-controlled than others. Before you make any firm decision about what you will store in your garage, you need to assess the following conditions to determine whether your things can be stored safely:

- Humidity levels
- Temperature extremes
- Susceptibility to water

Depending on where you live, temperatures in your garage can easily exceed 120 degrees in the summer. Is this where you want to store your candles, furniture, your old wedding dress, and other family heirlooms?

Some garages are insulated or have heating and cooling systems to varying degrees. If your garage is outfitted with such a system, you will have more options available to you as to what can be stored safely, and you will not need to be as concerned about things getting ruined. However, most of us are not so lucky and probably couldn't even afford the added utility expense to operate the heating and cooling systems even if we did have them. If your ability to store and use your garage is being inhibited by these factors, here are a few ideas to make

caution If you live in a humid climate, you will *not* want to store photographs, important papers, and clothing in your garage for long periods of time because they will mildew. I would encourage you to store photographs in archival boxes on the upper shelves of a closet in the house rather than taking a chance on storing them in the garage, even for a short period of time. If you decide to do so anyway, you should invest in air-tight containers that keep out the moisture.

caution If water has a tendency to back up into your garage when it rains, do not place anything of value or anything that is not water resistant on the floor. You will want to keep everything off the floor on shelves, in cabinets, or on wooden pallets to avoid water damage.

your garage more comfortable and user friendly as well as to broaden your storage options in hotter climates without breaking the bank:

Purchase a dehumidifier and run a tube to the outside of your garage for the water to drain. Otherwise, you will need to empty the reservoir every day and run the risk of it overflowing on your garage floor. Be sure to periodically inspect the tubing for signs of blockage.

Install a ceiling fan to circulate air. It can even be an old one you removed from the house when you remodeled. You will be surprised at what a huge difference this can make.

Consider having additional windows installed for more light and to improve cross-ventilation.

To do list

- ❑ Clarify your storage needs.
- ❑ Assess what you are currently storing.
- ❑ Decide how to use your garage storage space.
- ❑ Create a storage plan.

Determining Your Objective

Let's think about how you would like to use your garage from this point forward and what factors are important to consider before you can create a new design.

How do you want to be able to use your garage space? Be clear with yourself about your needs and the goal you are working toward. Are you a handyman who likes to build things, or is gardening your passion? If you have anything but a green thumb, then ask yourself if you really need to hang on to all those gardening tools and the 50 or so flower pots you have collected over the years. Likewise, if do-it-yourself projects are not your thing, you can consider reducing the size of your workbench and the number of tools you own.

Take a moment to consider whether the garage is truly the best place to store some of the things you have been keeping there. As you learned in the previous section of this chapter, some things are appropriate to store in the garage, and other things aren't. It is certainly not the place to store priceless heirlooms, nor does it make sense to pack it full of a bunch of worthless items that never get used, right?

However, the most important decision to be made at this point is whether you plan to park a car or two in the garage. Obviously, this is going to greatly influence and have the most significant impact on how much room will be left for the storage of other items.

Inventorying Your Garage Contents

Taking an inventory of the things you are currently storing in your garage will assist you in assessing your needs and creating your garage plan. Use the Garage Inventory in Table 1.1 or create your own form. Review the list and check off the items you own and need to provide room for in your garage plan. Notice that I said *need*, because it is likely that some of these items can go or be stored somewhere else.

If you have more than one of each item, insert a number in the blank. If you know that you need to get rid of some of these items by tossing them, donating them to charity or selling them, put an "X" in the blank or circle the item, and be sure to read Chapter 13, "Getting Rid of Stuff." Although this list is not exhaustive, it includes the larger items people often store in their garages, and there is space for you to add other essential items as well.

Table 1.1   Garage Inventory

_____ car(s)	_____ spare tire
_____ patio furniture	_____ workbench
_____ filing cabinet	_____ trash cans
_____ car seat	_____ lawn mower
_____ lawn chairs	_____ compressor
_____ washer	_____ skis
_____ dryer	_____ motorcycle
_____ refrigerator	_____ bicycle
_____ freezer	_____ scooter
_____ folding table	_____ weed eater
_____ folding chairs	_____ ladders
_____ luggage	_____ holiday decorations
_____ boat	_____ snow blower

Table 1.1   Continued

_____ canoe/kayak	_____ large power tools
_____ camping equipment	_____ lumber
_____ barbeque grill	_____ computer equipment
_____ propane tanks	_____ recycling containers
_____ boxed records	_____ memorabilia
_____ pool equipment	_____ furniture
_____ bookshelves	_____ fans
_____ outdoor games	_____ firewood
_____ pet supplies	_____ household supplies
_____ shoes	_____ wheelbarrow

Determining Whether Your Goal Is Realistic

Now, look at your list and ask yourself whether it is realistic to think that all this will fit within your newly organized garage, given the amount of space you have. Are you honestly going to have enough room to be able to park your cars and keep all this stuff in your garage, or do you need to consider getting a shed, securing offsite storage, or getting rid of some stuff? If so, you will want to be sure to read Chapter 5, "Analyzing Alternative Storage Solutions," as well as Chapter 13, "Getting Rid of Stuff," and Chapter 14, "Having a Successful Garage Sale."

You might not know the answers to these questions right now and will not know them until you are well into the organizing process. The last thing I want you to do, at this point, is to rush out and buy a shed because you think you need it and then fill it up with a bunch of stuff you don't need like you did in your garage. Nor do I want you to get an offsite storage unit and fill it with the contents of your garage. If you are not sure everything will fit in your garage, even when it is organized, I highly recommend that you wait until you have completed your garage-organizing project and are convinced that there is no other option before you secure additional storage.

Deciding What Stays and What Goes

If your garage is like most, not only has it become the place where you dump everything that you don't know what to do with, but it has become the personal dumping ground for everyone else in your family. If you can't find a home for something or are not quite ready to give it away, it ends up in the garage.

This is why the garage becomes the most clutter-filled room of the house. It is so much easier to store an item in the garage and put the decision off about what to do with it until later than to decide right now. Unfortunately, if you do this long enough, the thought of organizing the garage becomes a monumental undertaking rather than something that can be managed easily.

Satisfying Everybody's Needs

One of the reasons that makes garage organization so elusive is that this room serves the needs of everyone who lives in your house. This is less of a problem inside the house because everyone has his or her own space in addition to the common living area. At the very least, each family member has his or her own bedroom (or shares a bedroom), with allotted space to store individual clothing and other personal items such as toys, books, pictures, and so on. All the things we utilize to eat are stored in the kitchen, and most of the things we use to amuse and entertain ourselves are stored in the family room or game room.

It is all those other things that you don't know what to do with or no longer have use for that end up in the garage and complicate your mission to keep it organized. It is home to your children's bicycles and toys, lawn furniture, hardware, gadgets, family treasures, paint, crafts, and whole host of other items there just isn't any other logical place for. So, they end up in the garage.

How do you satisfy everybody? To use your garage to its best advantage, you need to understand that it can serve most of the needs of everyone living in the house within reason, but some hard choices must be made. You need to be realistic about what you can store in the garage and what you can't. You might love to camp out, but if your family has not gone camping for the past three years, perhaps it is time to part with some of that equipment. You might have the most extensive collection of holiday decorations ever assembled, but if you never bother to put them up, what is the sense of having them?

Paring Down Your List of Items to Be Stored

Chapter 2, "Understanding the Organizing Process," will give you in-depth guidance in reducing the amount of stuff you hold onto, but it is not too early to begin thinking about the things you no longer need. Hopefully, you already began to identify some of these items when you were completing Table 1.1. If you didn't, now would be a good time to review your list and identify any items you could get rid of.

Some people refer to this first step of the organizing process as the "gross sort." These are the quick-and-easy decisions you can make with little thought. It shouldn't take much deliberation to part with broken or unsafe equipment, dried-up paint, or things you haven't used in years. By making these types of decisions now, it will greatly simplify and speed up the rest of the organizing process. If you find this part of the process to be difficult, don't worry. You will learn many useful techniques to help you make these decisions in the next chapter and throughout the book.

Envisioning the Finished Product

You would not take a trip in the car without knowing where you were headed, nor would you buy new bedroom furniture without knowing the size of your bedroom. The same holds true when organizing your garage. You need to know where the major storage centers will be located, as well as other large items such as appliances, bicycles, and large power tools. Undoubtedly, some of your initial thoughts might change as you work through the process, but if you start with a rough plan, you will be able to accomplish this project in less time and are much more likely to be satisfied with the end result. In addition, this plan will serve as your "roadmap" to guide you through the process.

Study the sample garage layout shown in Figure 1.1 and identify the similarities and differences from your current layout. Using this sketch as a guide, analyze your current garage layout and how it could be improved. Ask yourself what is working and what is not.

Earlier in this chapter, you began to analyze how you have been using your garage and how you might want to use it differently in the future. Think about how you want your new garage layout to look. Using Figure 1.1 as a guide, create and sketch a plan that identifies the kinds of items you want to store in each area and label it to indicate where they will go. The chapter titles in Part II of this book will give you some ideas of particular storage centers you might need in your garage.

If you have a large quantity of a particular type of item, you will want to create a storage area so you can keep all those similar items together. However, if you have only a couple miscellaneous items of any particular type, you would not need to designate a special area in which to store them. This is just a rough plan to help you get started and begin thinking about where the best places are to store things in your garage. You will undoubtedly make modifications to your plan as you progress through the organizing process, but you have to start somewhere.

Don't be overly concerned with the method of storage you will use in each area—this will be discussed further in Chapter 3, "Reviewing Storage Options." However, it is important to consider the locations of windows and electrical outlets, doors to the house, and service doors in order to create the best possible layout (see Figure 1.2). It is important to locate your workbench near a power source for tools and lighting. Also, if your garage has windows, this will provide an excellent additional source of light to work on projects during the day.

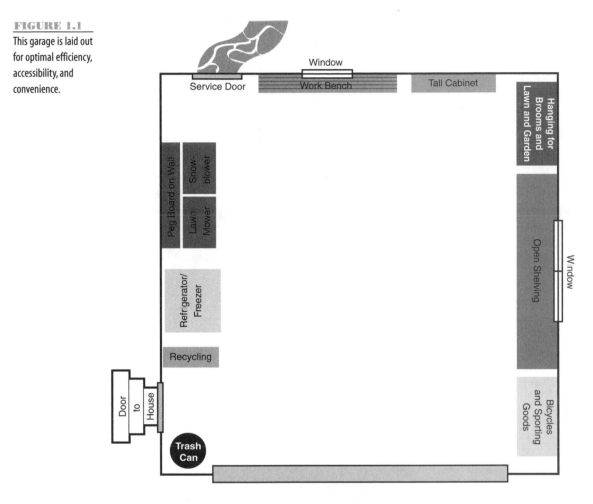

Sample Garage Plan

Your Garage Plan

Affording easy and convenient access to items and how often they are actually used
will also be important considerations in deciding where to store them. The more
something is used, the easier it should be to get to. Garbage cans and recycling bins
are best located somewhere between the door to the house and the door to the outside. Seasonal items can be stored up and out of the way, whereas tools and frequently used items should be close at hand.

You will also find it helpful to refer to your "Garage Inventory" so you don't leave
anything out.

To do list

- ☐ Establish a realistic timeframe.
- ☐ Identify individual project tasks.
- ☐ Ask family members and friends for assistance.

Creating a Plan for the Process

One of the first questions clients ask when they undertake their garage organizing project is, "How long is this going to take?" My answer is always the same, "I don't know how much stuff you have or how fast you can make decisions." If you are already able to park two cars in your garage, this is going to go a lot faster than if you have 20 years of accumulation strewn about here, there, and everywhere.

A lot will depend on how ruthless you will be in making decisions about what should be kept and what should be given away or tossed. You are going to have hundreds of decisions to make, and if each one takes five minutes, you can see how quickly the time will add up. In the next chapter, we will discuss the basic questions to ask yourself to speed up the decision-making process. The good news is that once you gain some momentum, I can assure you that these decisions will get easier to make and you will quickly become a pro at this. It just takes a while to get into the swing of things.

Breaking It Down into Small, Manageable Pieces

We have all heard the riddle, "How do you eat an elephant?" The answer: "One bite at a time." The same approach holds true for your garage. One of the cardinal rules for any organizing project you undertake is to break the project down into small, manageable pieces. Simply put, this means that it is not wise for most of you to plan on tackling the entire project in one day. You will defeat yourself before you even get started! By breaking the job down, your goal becomes much more realistic and attainable.

If your garage contains 30 years of accumulation, it is unrealistic for you to set a goal of organizing the entire space in one day. Using your garage plan as a guide, break the task down by organizing one wall or storage center at a time. Some of you might need to break the task down even further into individual components within a storage area. As you read through Part II, this will become more evident as you begin to organize each storage center and the individual steps to the organizing process are explained.

Decide how much time you plan to spend on this project at any given time and choose a realistic task that can be completed within that designated timeframe. If you have only two hours, it would not be wise to empty the entire garage and expect to be able to put everything back in an orderly fashion. However, it would be very realistic and much more manageable to clean off the top of your workbench, organize your toolbox, or sort your paint supplies in that amount of time.

The amount of time a particular task takes will ultimately depend on the quantity of items you are working with. For some, sorting screws would be a 15-minute process, whereas for others this could take hours. You might be able to organize all your lawn and garden supplies in less than an hour, but this process could take an avid gardener days.

By organizing a specific storage center at a time and selecting an appropriate task to complete in the amount of time you have to complete it, you will see quick and steady progress and will not become disillusioned and frustrated. If you try to do too much and don't give yourself enough time, more than likely you will give up before you see this project through to completion. I am sure some of you know the feeling well.

tip Set a date by when you would like the project to be completed. Sometimes, a deadline such as donating unwanted items to a school rummage sale or an advertised neighborhood garage sale is a great incentive to keep you on task. Just don't plan to do the entire job the day before, because you will not be happy with the result.

Trite as this might sound, the most important thing to remember is that "Rome was not built in a day." Go easy on yourself and do the best you can in whatever time you can devote to this project. If it is two hours per week or one Saturday in a month, you will get through it and the garage of your dreams can be yours.

Enlisting the Help of Others

Another important factor that will have a significant impact on how fast you get this project done is enlisting the help of family members, a paid helper, or a professional organizer.

If you have a partner and children, why don't you consider making this a family project? Do not overlook your children as willing and able assistants. Remember, lots of this stuff is theirs and they can be enlisted to help sort and clean all kinds of things. You will be surprised how helpful they can be, especially if you seize this as an opportunity to help them earn money for something they want by offering to pay them.

Your spouse could be more willing to help than you think if that is what it takes to get the job done. You are probably thinking that this might be the surest way to end your relationship and that one of you might not survive the process—but not if you play it smart! Just work in different areas or on different tasks and try to stay out of each other's way. Remember, if the family contributed to creating the mess, the family might be the quickest, easiest resource for sorting it out.

Storing Things Safely

The garage is considered one of the most potentially dangerous areas in the home. It makes sense when you think about it—the garage is home to all kinds of toxic chemicals and lethal substances we do not want to keep in the house. In addition, there are all kinds of power tools, sharp objects, and implements, not to mention wasps and spiders, which will do more than just grab your attention if they bite you. You need to protect yourself and other members of your household from the dangers that lurk within.

Try not to buy more paint remover, herbicides, and other potentially harmful substances than you need for a project, so you won't have a lot left to store. This is not one of the areas where it makes sense to buy a larger size because it's "on sale." Try to get the smallest size you might possibly need, and if there isn't much left, consider tossing it. This could save your child's life.

Most garages are not childproof by any means, so until you've finished cleaning, organizing, and securing the contents of your garage, keep your young children out of there. Children are naturally curious, and this is one place where it is not safe to let them explore. Those piles of clutter are appealing to children, and it is too tempting for them to start climbing and take a serious fall.

As you begin to organize your garage, it is important for you to be aware of a number of garage storage safety tips that will make your garage a safer place for the entire family:

- Store paints, toxic chemicals, pesticides, and flammable liquids in their original containers, away from heaters, pilot lights, and other sources of flame—and preferably in a locked cabinet. If storing most things on open shelving, place these types of items on the upper shelves out of your children's reach.
- Heavier items need to be stored on lower shelves and lighter items on higher shelves to prevent injury.
- Store gasoline and propane tanks in a well-ventilated area in an approved container with the cover tightly closed, no less than 50 feet away from sources of heat or flame, including furnaces, hot water heaters, and appliances with pilot lights.
- Do not keep old batteries around because they leak and explode over time.
- Keep tools out of your children's reach and wear goggles when you use them. Not only could this save your eyes from harm, but it will also set a great example for your children.

- Store flammable items away from work areas where you will be using tools that produce sparks.
- Store ladders horizontally, not upright, so they can't tip over on your children or vehicles.

USE YOUR GARAGE SAFELY

Garage safety goes beyond safe storage. Remember these tips to make sure you're using your garage safely:

＊ Use rags to wipe up or sawdust to absorb spills promptly and dispose of them properly. Consider putting wipeable mats under your car.

＊ Never use a charcoal or gas grill inside the garage, regardless of whether the door is open or closed.

＊ Have a GFI outlet near the workbench to prevent shock while using power tools.

＊ Do not use power tools with frayed or tattered power cords, and never leave them plugged in.

＊ Wear long sleeves, long pants, and gloves when working in the garage, especially when handling toxic chemicals and pesticides. These compounds can be absorbed through the skin and cause liver damage. This clothing can also protect you from the serious consequences of a poisonous insect bite.

＊ Keep a well-stocked first-aid kit in the garage.

＊ Never warm up your car with the garage door closed because deadly fumes can escape into your home.

＊ Install smoke and carbon monoxide detectors and have a fire extinguisher readily available.

＊ Be sure the garage door is open to provide good ventilation when using stains and other chemicals that emit toxic fumes.

＊ Keep your garage door closed when you are not in it. Many valuable items are stolen from homes each year, not through forced entry, but because garage doors are left open. Make it a regular habit to immediately close and lock your garage door after you have exited from your car. By keeping the door closed, not only do you discourage human intruders, but you'll also help keep out other unwanted guests, such as raccoons, chipmunks, squirrels, and mice. And don't get into the habit of leaving the door unlocked between the house and the garage; doing so only makes it easier for any intruder to walk right into your house!

✳ Hang a mirror on the front wall of the garage facing you at eye level as you drive in. An inexpensive full-length mirror turned sideways works great. Sounds a bit vain, but hardly. This will enable you to view behind your car as you drive into your garage and see if anyone tries to follow you on foot into the garage uninvited. Many robberies and personal attacks occur in this manner, and this tip could save your life.

Lifting Safely

I wish I could tell you that organizing your garage is not a strenuous activity, but I would not be telling the truth. All those boxes and large items will need to be moved and sorted, and it will involve a lot of lifting and bending. I am not telling you this to talk you out of doing this project—you need to do it, but the last thing you want is to injure your back in the process.

Your back is the foundation and structure that balances and supports your body. A serious back injury will change your life forever, so why risk it? Take a few minutes to read these simple guidelines and use your head. Don't overdo it and lift things that are too heavy for you. It's not worth it. If you have to strain to pick up an item, it is too heavy for you to lift!

The best advice is to use a dolly whenever possible and to observe the basic rules of lifting:

- Make sure you have a clear path to move through.
- Stand as close as possible to the object you intend to lift.
- Bend at your knees, not at your waist, to pick up the object, as shown in Figures 1.3 and 1.4.
- Grip the object firmly and grasp opposite corners.
- Bring the load close to your body, as shown in Figures 1.5 and 1.6.
- Lift your head and shoulders first.
- Keep your back straight and use your legs to slowly push up.
- Carry the load between your shoulders and waist.
- Don't twist your body while carrying the load.
- Bend your knees to slowly lower the load, keeping your fingers out of the way.

FIGURE 1.3

Bend at the knees and hips, not at your waist.

FIGURE 1.4

Not this way.

FIGURE 1.5

Hold the load close to your body.

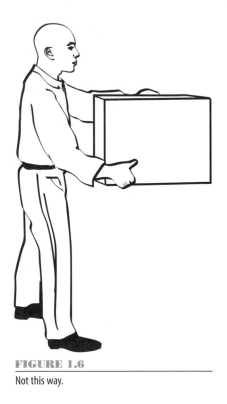

FIGURE 1.6

Not this way.

SHOULD I WEAR A BACK BELT WHILE LIFTING?

Wearing back belts to reduce injuries to the back has become a very controversial subject. The National Institute for Occupation Safety and Health concludes that there is insufficient scientific evidence supporting the claim that they actually do reduce back injuries. Although manufacturers maintain that they reduce spinal stress and restrict twisting movements, there are also concerns that those who wear them do so with a false sense of security and may actually subject themselves to a greater risk of injury. Though wearing a back belt could potentially be of some value and might very well live up to manufacturer claims, it is a personal choice and does not replace good common sense and adherence to accepted lifting safety guidelines.

Wearing a back belt is a personal choice.

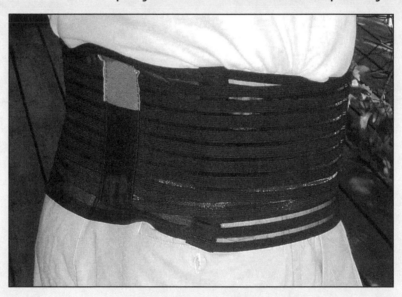

Summary

Now that you have analyzed your needs and have a picture in your mind and on paper of what you would like your garage layout to be and how it might look, what is the next step? Before you dive into this project, it is important to understand the basic steps of the organizing process. One of the reasons you have failed with this task in the past is that you did not have a systematic approach. In the next chapter, not only will you learn the basic organizing principles, but you will learn how to apply them to your particular situation.

Understanding the Organizing Process

The process of organizing your garage may seem so large and complex that you feel too overwhelmed to even begin. But in fact, the steps and techniques you learn in this chapter are very simple. What's more, you could already be doing some of them from time to time, without even realizing that you are taking strides toward total organization. By having an understanding of the basic organizational process up front, you can reduce your feeling of being overwhelmed and spend less time planning and accomplishing the project.

Whether you have decided that your entire garage needs attention or just a portion of it does, the organizing process will still be the same and the basic steps explained in this chapter will apply. In fact, the principles you learn here can be applied to any organizational process you undertake. By understanding these basic principles and steps in the organization process and why they are important, you will turn your garage-organizing project from an unpleasant experience you are dreading into a manageable, logical process you can master. You aren't expected to read this chapter and then go out and organize your garage; the information in this chapter is strictly given to provide you with an understanding and overview of the entire process you'll be undertaking. Later chapters of this book discuss in greater detail each of the steps and principles listed here. Think of this as your roadmap for the project ahead!

Remember, our goals are the same—to get your garage organized in the least amount of time with the least amount of effort. Learning the information in this chapter brings you one giant step closer to attaining that goal.

Choosing a Starting Point

As mentioned in Chapter 1, "Where Do I Begin?", one of the most important things you can do as you begin the process of organizing your garage is to break the project into small, doable pieces. In other words, do not tackle the entire garage at once.

When I work alongside clients inside their homes, we usually begin in the room that is bothering them the most or where the fastest visible results can be achieved, so they will experience the most immediate gratification possible.

note Even if you are determined to organize the entire garage in one day, you can still divide the project into identifiable steps or phases. This is an important part of the organizational process, so follow the guidelines you learn in this chapter, whatever the size of the project you're tackling.

The same thing holds true in the garage. It makes good sense to begin in an area that will give you a true feeling of accomplishment and motivate you to continue. Ideally, you would want to start in one section of the garage and work through it in a logical fashion. Where you choose to start will largely depend on the volume of stuff you have in your garage, the state in which that stuff is currently stored, and the area of your garage you would most like to have organized. If the family's sporting equipment is spread all over the garage and the house, you might decide that this would be a good place to start. Or if the Christmas decorations are still sitting in the middle of the garage floor and summer is approaching, getting those out of the way will give you a real boost.

I know what you might be thinking: "Barry's the expert, so he should tell me the best place to start." And you would be right to a certain degree. But even though I can guide you through the basic organizing principles, these principles can be applied in a multitude of ways, depending on the unique circumstances of each situation.

And, in some garages, there's simply no way to work in one area and then move to the next, because there is barely room to move at all. You see a perfect example of such a garage in Figure 2.1

FIGURE 2.1
Where do I begin?

Where is the most logical place to start here? In the back corner? Perhaps so, if you could maneuver your way back there. This garage holds a decade or more of accumulation, leaving little room to wade through it. When clutter reaches these epic proportions, it doesn't really matter where you start. For these situations, I recommend that you begin in the center and clear that area first as you work your way toward the outer walls. This approach immediately creates some work space and begins to reduce the volume.

If you are already parking cars in your garage, then it is more logical to start on the outer wall, working your way around the perimeter, one section at a time. It really doesn't matter which section you begin with, so just choose a starting point based on what looks the most feasible and makes the most sense to you.

In deciding where to begin, choose a section that will give you the most pleasure and be the most gratifying and motivating to propel you through the rest of this project. You might choose to start with your workbench because you are always fixing one thing or another and can never seem to find the tools you need. That disorganized mess in the storage cabinet has been bothering you for months, and organizing it would make you feel like you're really getting somewhere. Or perhaps you should begin by going through that pile of stuff in the back corner where that offensive odor seems to be coming from! You really can't make a wrong choice here.

YOU AND YOUR SYSTEM MUST BE RIGHT FOR EACH OTHER

Before we get too far along, let me dispel an organizing myth. There is no right or wrong way to organize. The whole purpose of doing this in the first place—besides to make the garage look better—is to create a system that is going to work for you and with you. Your vision of the ideal garage is going to be totally different from mine, but that's not what matters. What is important is that when you are finished, you will be happy with the end result and be able to find what you want—when you need it. Will your system work and will you like it? And even more important, will you keep it up? That's what matters!

To do list

- ☐ Eliminate items that require little thought.
- ☐ Group the purged items into piles.
- ☐ Rent a dumpster (if necessary).

Reducing the Volume: Making the Easy Decisions

In Chapter 3, "Reviewing Storage Options," and Chapter 4, "Selecting Storage Systems," you learn how to choose and set up an organizational system for your garage. However, before you can choose a system, you need to know what kind of volume you are dealing with. It is important to go through and cull out the items you know you don't want to keep, early in the organizing process, so you know just what you have to store. Your needs could be drastically different from what you had originally imagined once you have completed the sorting and elimination process.

Therefore, the first step of the garage-organizing process is what I refer to as "reducing the volume" or a "gross sort." What does that mean exactly? It means making the simple and easy decisions first and eliminating as much stuff as you can—as fast as you can. It will give you an immediate lift, a great feeling of accomplishment, and help you clearly see what is left to deal with. This serves two purposes:

- It will better enable you to select the appropriate system for your needs.
- It will give you an accurate sense of what you need to create space for.

Things You'll Need

- ❑ Cardboard boxes
- ❑ Trash can
- ❑ Heavy-duty trash bags
- ❑ Work gloves (if desired)
- ❑ Dumpster (if necessary)

So, how do you do this? Take a quick look around and immediately weed out the items that can easily be tossed or given away. What about that baby stroller, which hasn't been used in four years, the six boxes of 10-year-old *National Geographic* magazines, the broken VCR, the three old pairs of skis (one with broken bindings), the crate from when your four-year-old German Shepherd was a puppy, and the almost-new treadmill, which seemed like a good idea at the time, but is now simply gathering dust?

As you begin to discard the items, sort them into three piles: one pile for the items that are obviously trash, another pile for items you want to sell, and a third pile for the stuff you want to donate. If your garage is crammed full of stuff, begin making these piles outside on the driveway. This is an ideal place because you won't run out of space and you can quickly get this stuff out of your way as you create some room to move around inside the garage. If you are already able to park cars in your garage, back them out and you can make the piles in the center of the garage for now and deal with them later.

Depending on the volume of stuff you will be discarding during this initial stage of the organizing process, you might find it easier just to leave everything in piles until you are finished with this step. If you have a large, heavy-duty trash can on wheels, toss the trash directly into it. If not, or when it becomes full, line another trash can or box with a heavy-duty trash bag that can easily be removed as it becomes full. Trash bags are not only good for trash, but will work well for things you want to donate or sell. Just be sure to label the bags of stuff you want to donate or sell and keep them separate from the trash bags. Otherwise, you could easily get confused about what is in each bag as they start to accumulate all around you. Use the empty cardboard boxes for the more fragile stuff you plan to sell or donate. For more information on how to sell or where to donate your discarded items, see Chapter 13, "Getting Rid of Stuff."

Your goal now is to get through this part of the process quickly and make only fast-and-easy decisions. The idea is to get as much cleared out as quickly as possible. Now is not the time to sort screws or plumbing parts. If you come across a box of old papers or mementos that need to be carefully gone through, put them aside and save that for later. You will be amazed at how quickly you will begin to see visible progress if you don't let yourself get bogged down with the small stuff at first.

You might have 23 half-gallon cans of paint in your garage and think that you need lots of shelf space or a special cabinet just to accommodate them all. Once you complete the initial sorting and weeding process, you will undoubtedly discover that eight of the cans have dried up or are empty, six are from the previous owner or are colors no longer being used in your house, three are unidentifiable, and only six cans you need to keep. So, in this case, you would have easily misjudged your storage requirements and made some poor choices.

tip Later on, you're going to learn a lot about storing your goods in containers. Though you may have to buy many of these containers, you might have some lying about right under your nose. As you're discarding items, you'll want to be sure to keep those that can be used to efficiently containerize the things you keep. Be sure to see the sidebar later in this chapter, "Use the Containers You Have," for more information on this topic.

What sense does it make to create the capacity to store six bicycles when the reality is that only two of them are being used and the other four have been outgrown or are broken? The same thing holds true for your camping equipment. Why keep it if you haven't been camping for four years and have no intention of ever sleeping in a tent again?

Consider a dumpster if you anticipate large amounts of trash.

RENTING A DUMPSTER

If you are dealing with decades of garage clutter, your garbage can might be sorely inadequate for the amount of trash this project will generate. Having a dumpster delivered to accommodate the volume you are likely to toss will be a lifesaver and well worth the additional cost, especially if you are getting rid of a lot of large, heavy, and bulky items or decades of accumulation. Who wants to look at all those trash bags while you are funneling them out with your weekly trash or waiting for a scheduled heavy trash pickup? Dumpsters are available in a variety of sizes, and the delivery company will help you determine the size you need.

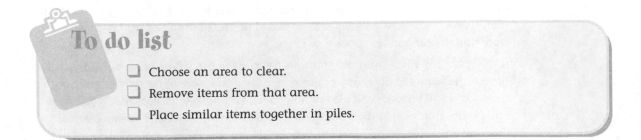

To do list

- ❑ Choose an area to clear.
- ❑ Remove items from that area.
- ❑ Place similar items together in piles.

Removing Items and Clearing Space

Once you have completed a gross sort, hopefully you will have reduced the volume and created some room to move around. I need to warn you that things might very well look a bit worse before they start to look better, but I assure you that this is part of the process. At this point, you have piles of trash, trash in bags, items to sell or donate, and stuff you're still not sure about. The mess has become a bit more spread out, but don't be concerned about that right now, as this is quite normal. The important thing is that you keep moving through the process and continue to make progress.

You are now ready to select an area to begin the actual organizing process. This can mean removing one box from the center of the garage, all of the items within or on a particular shelf in a cabinet, or an assortment of items that are stacked in the corner.

Things You'll Need

- ❑ Your garage plan
- ❑ Cardboard boxes
- ❑ Heavy-duty trash bags
- ❑ Clear space to make piles

Clearing Area by Area

To clear a space for the items that will be assigned to it, you need to remove what is there and create a home. Just as you and I need a place to live, so do the items stored in your garage. The home you select for each item will depend on many factors, which will be discussed extensively in Chapter 3. In Chapter 1, you created a rough plan and decided where you would like these homes to be. This will be a valuable tool when you actually begin to organize because you will have already

thought this through. Of course, you will undoubtedly make some revisions to your plan as you move through the process based on the quantity of stuff you need to store and the amount of space you have.

If the space you're clearing will continue to store the same type of items, you might have some sense of how many of those items you can store in that area. In other words, you will have a good idea of how much you have to dispose of. If you have more space than you know what to do with, you aren't faced with the problem of deciding what to keep and what to toss. But if you are like most, you will want to keep much more than you have room for, and these decisions will be more challenging.

As you clear items from the storage area and are reasonably sure you will store them in the same area, you can just lay them to the side or in the middle of the garage floor, out of your way for sorting. They won't be there long because you will be returning these items to their home immediately after they have been sorted. However, if all or some of the items removed will not be returned to and stored in the same place, move them to the area where other items of this type are currently being stored. If that is not possible, just box them up and put them aside for now.

Clearing the Entire Garage

If you're among those brave souls whose plan is to accomplish the bulk of this project in one day (and you think that this goal is realistic), you might decide to remove everything from the garage or large sections of it. In that situation, you might choose to haul everything out to the driveway at one time to begin the sorting process, as shown in Figure 2.2.

FIGURE 2.2

The removal process. (Photo courtesy of Sensible Organizing Solutions.)

As a matter of fact, you can get a head start on the sorting process if you will begin to group like things together as you carry them out, as shown in Figure 2.3. Your lawn and garden tools might be all over the garage right now, but if you can group them together in a pile on the driveway or in the middle of the garage, this will save you lots of time later. The same thing applies to your sporting goods and any other type of item you have a lot of. Refer to your garage plan to remind yourself what your storage groups will be or review the chapter headings in Part II of this book for some good suggestions.

FIGURE 2.3
Getting stuff out will help the sorting stage of the removal process. (Photo courtesy of Center for Organization and Goal Planning.)

Just be sure that you have enough time and that your goal is reasonable. Who knows; if you're lucky, people will think you are having a garage sale and you can sell some of your stuff without having to put it back! Do not drag out more than you can deal with in the time you have allotted. Otherwise, you might just have to drag it all back in because you didn't have enough time. Remember, all the items you drag out need to be thoroughly sorted and culled, and the storage area needs to be prepared for their return.

HOW LONG IS THIS GOING TO TAKE?

In Chapter 1, I told you that one of the first questions potential clients ask me about any organizing project is, "How long is this going to take?" I also told you that my answer is always the same: "I don't know how much stuff you have and how fast you can make decisions." These are two critical factors in assessing how long any organizing job will take.

I also remind people that they didn't create this mess in a day and it is unlikely that they will be able to alleviate it in one day either. For many, garage clutter represents years of accumulation and decisions that have not been made. If your garage has 20 years of accumulation and you are going to ponder getting rid of each and every item for five minutes, I think you can easily see how the time will add up quickly and this could slow your progress.

In addition, remember that organizing your garage is a bit more strenuous than organizing your pantry or bedroom closet. More than likely, you are going to be doing a lot of lifting, and many of the items stored out there are heavy. If you are not in the best of health or you have chosen to begin this project on a hot summer day, your stamina will be a contributing factor as to how long this will take. All the more reason for you to try and enlist the help of your family or friends, as discussed earlier.

If you are unsure about how much you can accomplish in the amount of time you have set aside for this project, start small and work with the items in one storage area at a time. If your garage does not yet have any designated storage centers, begin with a box, a shelf, or a cabinet and see how far you get. As you move through the process, you will get better at predicting how long the various steps of this process will take.

To do list

- ❑ Gather items to be sorted.
- ❑ Sort items by type.
- ❑ Group similar items together.

Sorting Things Out

The official dictionary definition of the word *sort* is "to arrange and put things into categories according to their shared attributes." In other words, putting like things together. Sorting is the first step in the organizing process of deciding what you want to keep and what you want to get rid of.

The purpose of the sorting process is two-fold:

- It helps you determine the quantity of a particular type of item you have.
- It facilitates the purging and weeding process.

tip Once the items have been removed from the garage or one area of the garage, clean the space you've just cleared. If you cleared the floor, take this opportunity to sweep; if you cleared a shelf, wipe it off. Who knows when you will have this cleaning opportunity again.

If you don't know how many or how much of something you have, there is little way to make an informed decision about what you want to keep. Obviously, you won't know that you should consider getting rid of some screwdrivers until you gather and sort them all, only to realize that you have 36 of them. At the point, when you see all 36 of them laid out, you will realize that you more than likely don't need that many. Figures 2.4 and 2.5 illustrate this point.

FIGURE 2.4

When you initially sort items into major categories, you are able to determine how large a single group might be, but you might not know whether you need everything in that group.

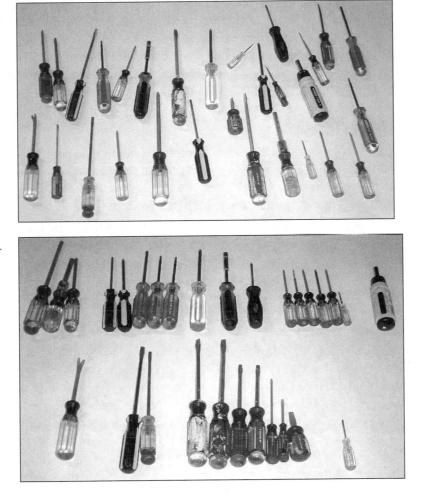

FIGURE 2.5

After the sorting process, you're better able to determine what you want to keep and what you can get rid of.

Things You'll Need

- ☐ Items to be sorted
- ☐ A flat sorting surface
- ☐ Labeled cardboard boxes

So how do you sort? You divide and group your things into major categories and types: electrical supplies, plumbing supplies, painting supplies, tools, sporting goods, lawn and garden.

Once you have completed this first phase, you more than likely will need to sort again within a specific category, such as tools, and subdivide into screwdrivers, hammers, and wrenches. The best way is to lay everything out (and, yes, you will need some space to do this). If you are just getting started and your garage is crammed full, you will need to begin this process on the garage floor or out on the driveway. The important thing is to be able to see what you have in order to analyze and make the important decisions about what you can live without. Everyone's needs are different in regard to how much or how many of something he or she thinks is necessary to have.

Grouping Like Things Together

A major component of the sorting process is grouping like things together. This helps you understand the quantity of any particular item you have and makes it easier to determine what to get rid of. When you return these sorted items to their new, well-organized "home," you'll store them in labeled boxes as well.

Think of your garage as a mini hardware store. In a hardware store, items are grouped together in a particular aisle or section of the store by the type of item they are. This is done because it makes finding something so much easier for the consumer. Imagine what shopping at a hardware store—or any store for that matter—would be like if there was no order and the hammers were at one end of the store and the screwdrivers were at the opposite end. What a frustrating shopping experience that would be!

The same holds true in your garage. When you store like things together, you know where to go when you need something, and this saves you time. It is elementary really. Whether you need a Phillips head screwdriver or a can of spray paint, isn't it easier to have all your screwdrivers in one place sorted by type and have all the cans of spray paint together in another? If you are looking for a particular size of wood screw, it is much easier to find it if the screws are separated from the nails and the bolts, right? It makes good sense to store paint brushes, rollers, and drop cloths with the paint. If these items are all in one place, you save yourself time when you are ready to begin a painting project.

Begin with several large boxes labeled "Toss," "Donate," and "Garage Sale" (if you plan to have one), and have several other "Keep" boxes labeled by category (see Figure 2.6). If you are sorting large, bulky items, boxes might not be suitable and you will need to section off the driveway and make piles instead. Keep in mind that whatever you drag out to the driveway will need to be brought back in at the end of the day.

FIGURE 2.6
Use labeled boxes to sort your goods into like groups.

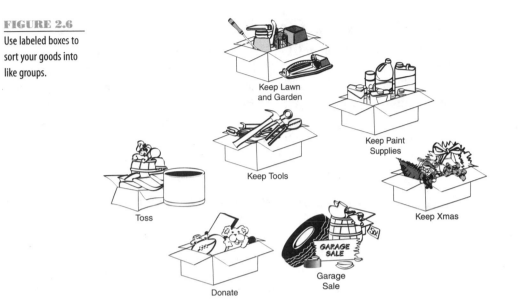

Keep Lawn
and Garden

Keep Paint
Supplies

Keep Tools

Toss

Keep Xmas

Garage
Sale

Donate

Creating Subgroups of Like Things

When sorting some categories of items, such as plumbing supplies, you might decide that storing them all in the same container is enough and that no further sorting is necessary. This will depend on the quantity you have of a particular type of item. The more you have of a particular item, the more detailed you will need to be in the sorting process—and the longer it will take. If you know how to perform major plumbing repairs and have collected a lot of pieces and parts over the years, you will want to sort them by type, containerize them in storage boxes of the appropriate size, and label them well.

caution Using the driveway or yard to sort items removed from the garage works just fine, but always be sure to check the weather forecast before you begin hauling stuff outside. You don't want to find yourself working in the rain as your sorting boxes and possessions become soaked.

To do list

- ☐ Eliminate items you no longer need.
- ☐ Determine how you will get rid of them.

Deciding What to Get Rid Of

When you first began this organizing project, you got rid of a number of items you could immediately identify as "disposable." Now, as you work through the sorting process, you will undoubtedly find more things you can toss or give away. This is the part of the organizing process that is referred to as *purging* or *weeding*. For some, this will naturally occur as an integral and simultaneous part of the sorting process, and for others, it will not occur until after everything has been sorted. The important thing is not when this happens, but that it happens at some point!

So, how do you decide what to keep, what to donate, and what to toss?

You know that you don't need all this stuff, but for one reason or another you resist and hold onto it. Having all this stuff makes you feel good, but is it really necessary for you to have a mini version of Home Depot in your garage?

You will be surprised at all the things you will find buried deep within, and there is no doubt that eventually you will readily see how ridiculous it would be to hold on to them. Some things will be more difficult to part with than others, however. There is no doubt about that.

Broken, obsolete, and rusty things that you don't use anymore should be an easy toss. And I don't want to hear, "But this is a good handle!" Maybe so, but I'm sure there is someone out there who needs a "good handle" more than you do. What you need to do right now is "get a handle" on what is really important to keep and what is just taking up space.

Making the Hard Decisions on What to Keep or Toss

People will always have their reasons as to why they cannot part with something, and I am the first one to admit that some of these reasons are valid—and some are not. Trust me, I have heard every excuse in the book as to why someone can't get rid of something. Here are some of the most common:

- **I might need it someday**—That could very well be true, but if you haven't used it up to now, what makes you think you will ever really need it someday? And if it's taking up a lot of space, isn't it worth taking the chance that you'll be able to live without it?

- **I could use it for parts**—Perhaps so, if you could remember that you have it or could find it when and if that time ever comes. Unless the piece is incredibly valuable, useful, and difficult to replace, is storing it worth your trouble?

- **I paid a lot of money for it**—Now, how relevant is that argument, as the item sits there gathering dust, taking up valuable space, and you have not gotten around to using it in the three years since you bought it? If you're unlikely to ever use the item, offer it for sale or donate it and take the value as a tax deduction (following the rules for such deductions, of course). See Chapter 13.

- **Uncle John gave it to me**—I could understand being sentimental about Uncle John's watch or his cuff links, but don't you think even he would wonder why you are holding on to his rusty toolbox with a broken lock, which he very well might have bought in a garage sale himself?

Don't get the wrong idea. Only you can decide whether something is worth keeping. I would never think of urging you to get rid of something you need against your will. My job is to identify the tough questions you should ask yourself so you can make the best decision for you. If you have plenty of space, this will be less of an issue for you.

When I'm helping clients come to grips with the difficult task of "letting go" of things they no longer need, asking the following list of questions[1] makes it easier for them to reach a decision:

- When was the last time you used it? Better yet, have you ever used it? Consider all the things you have in your garage you have never used. Can you really justify having this item occupy so much space for the one time five years from now that you might foresee a use for it? You know, there is always the option of renting a tool or borrowing one from your neighbor. A good rule of thumb is that if you haven't used something in the last two years, it's a goner.

- Is the item in good working condition and safe to keep? If it's not, why would you even consider keeping it? If you are thinking about holding on to a power tool with a frayed or tattered power cord, don't—unless you plan on having it professionally repaired. And let's be realistic here. How long will it take for you to get that accomplished? If the tool emits sparks, it's a fire hazard and should be discarded.

- Is it something that is still useful and relevant? Of course it was when you bought it, but you are going to find things lurking in your garage that have certainly outlived their usefulness. Like the electric hedge trimmer you brought to the new house without realizing that you don't have any bushes to trim, or the carpet remnant from the carpet that used to be in the family room before you installed ceramic tile. And what about that leftover lumber from when you had the backyard deck installed three years ago, or the 10-year-old floor polisher you used in your former house to polish the terrazzo?

[1]   Questions were inspired by Barbara Hemphill's "The Art of Wastebasketry®".

I am not saying that these things are no longer valuable to someone, but there is a good chance that person is no longer you. Just because something is still good, that doesn't mean you need to keep it for yourself.

- Do you have a logical place and enough space to keep it? I am sure there are many things you would like or would find useful to continue holding onto, but do you have the room? If it is something that would get very occasional use and your available space is limited, it is that much harder to justify keeping the item and having it take up valuable space that could be utilized for things used on a much more regular basis. You could consider giving it to a friend or neighbor who would use it much more often than you ever would. This way, you can just ask to borrow it for the occasional use you might have for it.

- What is the worst thing that will happen if you get rid of it? This is my favorite question! If you can live with your answer, by all means, get rid of it! Or simply said another way, "When in doubt, throw it out!"

Finding New Owners for Unwanted Items

As you are sorting and you decide that you want to get rid of something, your next decision is to determine whether someone else could use it or it needs to be tossed or recycled. Several chapters in this book explain how to dispose of items you no longer want or need. Here's a list of some possibilities and references to the chapters that discuss them in more detail:

- Obviously, if something is broken, in poor condition, no longer usable, or unsafe, no one else is going to want it either, and your only option is to toss or recycle it. You learn the details of that task in Chapter 13.

- For items that are toxic or are too cumbersome to deal with, you will also learn the various options available to dispose of them in Chapter 13.

- For the rest of the items you no longer wish to keep, more than likely you will want to donate them (see Chapter 13) or save them for a garage sale (see Chapter 14, "Having a Successful Garage Sale").

Selecting a Home

Everything needs a home in which to "live," and the items in your garage are no exception. Now that the items for a particular storage center are sorted and you have eliminated everything you no longer need, the next step is to assign a home to every item you intend to keep. Your job is to select the most suitable, logical, and convenient place for those items to be stored.

Chapters 3 and 4 explore selecting the best home for various types of items. But the general rule of thumb is that you want to store like things together in a safe and accessible place near where they will be used, so you can access those items safely, easily, and conveniently. The most relevant considerations when choosing a storage location are as follows:

note Think of the homes you select for your possessions as permanent abodes. New items within a category go in that category's home; you return items to their homes after using them. That way, you will always know where something is when you need it, and you will be able to retrieve it quickly and easily. You know how frustrating it is not to be able to find something when you need it. You know that you have it somewhere, but can't find it to save your life. If you put something in the same place all the time, it will always be right where it belongs, and you'll never have to hunt for it again. Imagine how empowering that will be!

- The type, size, and weight of the item
- How often and where the item is used
- The safest way to store the item
- Which location provides easiest access

You wouldn't store your underwear in the dining room, would you? No, you would put it in a cabinet or drawer in your bedroom, so when you get dressed in the morning, it's exactly where you need it, right? This is why we store pots and pans near the stove in the kitchen, clothing in our closets, and laundry detergent near the washing machine.

By applying this same logic to the garage, it makes sense that your mops, brooms, cleaning supplies, recycle bins, and extra refrigerator (if you have one) should be located near the door to the house, as shown in Figure 2.7. The tools you use most often should be near the workbench, and the lawn and garden items should be conveniently located and readily accessible near the door through which they will be carried outside.

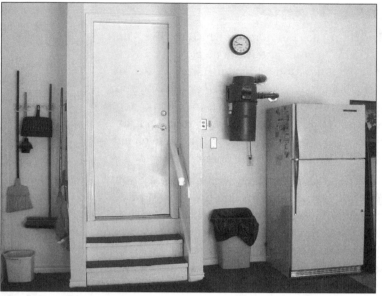

Containerizing Your Goods

When you reach the stage of your organizational process in which you are ready to store items in their new homes, it is often advisable to containerize them in some way. One of the main reasons for doing so is to ensure that like things stay together, so you don't have to repeat the entire sorting process six months from now. With so many people using these various items, storing them in containers makes it much easier to ensure they will be returned to their proper place.

Choosing the proper container depends on the item being stored in it. This topic is discussed in more detail in Part II, "Creating Storage Centers: Everything Needs a Home," as you begin to set up your individual storage centers. The major considerations for choosing containers include the following:

- Size
- Durability
- Cost
- Visibility of contents

Here again, there is no right or wrong way to containerize your possessions—the important thing is that you do it! You are not going to make tragic mistakes in choosing containers.

caution

Do not store hazardous and toxic substances in anything other than their original container with the appropriate precautionary labels. Never reuse the empty container, and be sure to read the label for proper disposal instructions.

There are many choices, and all can work well if labeled properly. The object is to get things into appropriate containers—they need to be functional, not fancy. Figures 2.8 and 2.9 show sample container storage systems.

FIGURE 2.8

Containers don't have to be fancy; they need to be functional.

FIGURE 2.9

The size of container used depends on what is being stored in it.

USE THE CONTAINERS YOU HAVE

As I mentioned earlier, before discarding any containers, cans, or boxes from the house, I always assess whether they can be used to store something in the garage. It often doesn't matter whether you can see through it, as long as you label it. There are many things you might already have that can be used to containerize items in the garage, including margarine and yogurt containers, jars, coffee cans, cookie tins, wash tubs, plastic cups with lids, Tupperware®, plastic or cardboard shoe boxes, Ziploc® bags, small buckets, old trash cans, milk crates, wooden boxes, baskets, old jewelry boxes, copy paper boxes with lids, and silverware drawer dividers.

Be careful not to take this suggestion so literally that you resolve never to throw another container away again just because "you might need it someday." You certainly don't need 37 margarine containers and 27 coffee cans. Keeping a half dozen or so of anything on hand is fine, but until you figure out how you are going to use those items, you can afford to discard the rest. And the good news is, there will always be more where those came from.

To do list

- ❑ Create labels to know what's inside.
- ❑ Determine the best labeling method for you.
- ❑ Purchase a label maker (if desired).

Labeling the Contents

Labeling is the important final step in the organizing process. Simply put, labeling your storage containers helps you identify and find things easier. Labels are especially important on containers you can't see through. Nothing is more frustrating than having to open several boxes or containers to find what you are looking for, when you could have found it on the first try if you had only labeled the container first. Labeling also makes it much easier to put things back in their proper place because there is no guesswork involved, especially if you have removed items from several different boxes (see Figure 2.10). It is a good idea to clearly label fragile items to remind you to be extra careful with that container the next time you handle it.

If you have lots of items in large boxes, you might consider creating a basic indexing system. In addition to the descriptive label, assign a number to the box or container. Then, keep a list or index card file of the box numbers and exactly what items are contained inside. This system will prove invaluable and save you a lot of time when you are looking for something specific and can't remember which box it is in.

Ways to Label

You have several different ways to label your storage boxes and containers. Whichever way you choose, be sure that the label is visible and placed on the side of the container that faces out.

The simplest and certainly the most cost-effective way to label something is by using a permanent marker and writing directly on the box or container itself. Although not the prettiest option, it serves the purpose. If you prefer not to write directly on the container, place a piece of masking tape on the container and write on the tape itself. However, over time, the tape could lose its adhesiveness and might come off. Mailing labels also work well for this purpose.

Another labeling technique is to attach a picture of the item contained inside to the outside of the box or container. This can be an actual photograph taken with a digital or 35mm camera or a picture that has been cut out from the original box or wrapper.

Using a Label Maker

Label makers have come a long way since the days of creating embossed labels with handheld devices, where a person had to turn a dial and punch in each letter individually. Though embossed label makers are still used today, the handheld and desktop electronic types have quickly gained a huge share of the label maker market. An even newer entrant to the label maker scene is the type that attaches to your computer. Three of the major manufacturers of label makers are Brother (www.brother.com), Casio (www.casio.com), and Dymo (www.dymo.com). A Brother handheld label maker is shown in Figure 2.11; Figure 2.12 shows a Casio model, and the Dymo Label Writer is shown in Figure 2.13.

FIGURE 2.11

A Brother handheld model label maker.

FIGURE 2.12

The Casio desktop model.

FIGURE 2.13

Dymo Label Writer. (Photo courtesy of Esselte.)

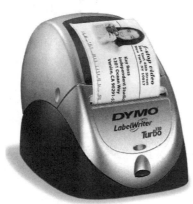

Label makers come in all shapes, sizes, and price ranges, creating labels in many sizes and colors. They are readily available at major office supply stores, and you will find a multitude of features offered.

Here is a list of some of the more important considerations when buying a label maker. In general, as the price goes up, so does the number of options.

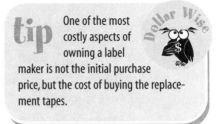

tip One of the most costly aspects of owning a label maker is not the initial purchase price, but the cost of buying the replacement tapes.

- **Tape size**—How many sizes of labels do you need?
- **Font style and size**—Is a choice of style or size of the letters important to you?
- **Type style**—Will normal and bold type suit your needs or is the ability to make labels with italic, shadowed, or boxed lettering important to you?
- **Number of lines of text printed**—Do you need the ability to print more than one line of text on a label?
- **Horizontal and vertical printing**—Is the option of printing labels vertically important?

Of course, the more you are willing to spend, the more bells and whistles your label maker will have. Consider what you are going to use your label maker for and remember that, as with any purchase, bigger is not always better. Investigate the features that are most important to you and buy the one that meets your needs and is in your price range.

note Handheld and desktop label makers are commonly operated with batteries, but some include AC adapters.

To do list

- ❏ Return items to their home when you're done with them.
- ❏ Refine your system on an ongoing basis.

Maintaining Your System

What good will it do you to spend hours or days organizing your garage only for it to look the same or worse than it does right now within six months or less? This is one of the most critical, yet most overlooked, steps in the organizing process and where many people fail despite their best of intentions. What a waste of time and effort if the results are not going to last—agreed?

As important as having a garage that looks good is to you, even more important is having a garage that functions well. If your garage does not function well, it isn't going to look good for very long.

The best system in the world is not going to last very long if it is not convenient and efficient or if you don't have the discipline to keep it up. This means that you and the rest of your family must put things away in their designated homes when you are finished using them and resist your old behavior patterns of just setting things anywhere "for now." If you continue to load up your garage with things that you don't know where else to put, you will defeat your best effort and your success will not be long lasting.

In addition to requiring of you a true mental commitment to stick with your new system, the system must work well. It is important to evaluate your system continually and determine how it can be improved. If everything is working well except in one storage area, analyze what you could do differently to eliminate the problem. Does one storage area quickly deteriorate faster than another? If so, pay attention to the signs. This is an indication that you need to tweak the method or change the location. Consider why your system is breaking down. More than likely, you did not allot enough space for this particular storage center or make it convenient enough. Heed the warning and make the necessary changes before things get out of control.

With some perseverance and determination, not only can the garage of your dreams be yours today, but it can stay that way! Just stay on top of it, monitor your system, and be ready to make changes where necessary.

Summary

Hopefully you now have a fundamental grasp of the basic steps integral to the organizing process. I told you that they would be easy to understand. Now that I have identified them, you are almost ready to begin applying them. But first, it is important to spend a little more time on how to select the best home for each item. In the next chapter, you will learn the various considerations for deciding what to store where and how to determine whether to hang something or store it in a drawer, on an open shelf, or in a cabinet.

Reviewing Storage Options

The garage has long been treated as the stepchild of the house. Imagine a bedroom without a bed, a bathroom without a sink, or a kitchen without counters or cabinets. It just wouldn't work, would it? These essential elements ensure that the rooms in our home function properly and meet our needs. So, how can we expect to have organized garages with no cabinets or shelves to use? It just doesn't work. We consider ourselves lucky if our garage came with some pegboard already installed or the previous owner left some old shelving behind. That's a start for sure, but it certainly isn't enough if you want to keep your garage organized and maximize the use of your storage space.

The storage method you ultimately choose for your tools, sporting goods, paint supplies, or whatever else it is you are storing will depend on several factors:

- Your personal storage style
- The size of your garage
- The type and quantity of things you are storing
- The kind of storage systems you already own that can be utilized
- Your budget to purchase a new storage system

Some of these items will be discussed in this chapter and the remainder will be addressed in Chapter 4, "Selecting Storage Systems." In this chapter, you will determine whether you have lots to hang, store on the floor, drop in a drawer, or stack on a shelf. You will learn which method of storage is best suited to the types of things you are currently storing and analyze whether things you have traditionally hung could be better stored in a drawer or on a shelf, and vice versa. These decisions will depend in part on the storage systems you already have in place. You might just need to purchase one component to complement what you already have. In this chapter, you learn important options to consider when choosing a new storage system, so you can be certain to choose the one that will work best for you.

Assessing Your Storage Style

One of the basic rules for any organizing project is that there is more than one way to organize anything—there is no right or wrong way to do it. As mentioned in the previous chapter, good organization is about creating a system that works for you and sticking with it. The best organizing system in the world will not work if you don't keep it up. I have seen some of the crudest organizing systems work well when the person diligently sticks to the system and maintains it.

You might be wondering what this has to do with where you ultimately decide to put something in your garage—whether you are going to hang it up, shelve it, or put it in a drawer. The type of storage solution you choose often depends on the type of person you are. Your personal storage style refers to the way you see your world, how you like your things to be arranged, and what "convenient access" means to you.

Each of us has a different tolerance level for visual clutter and varying levels of comfort with how many of our possessions we want to see at one time when we are not using them. Some people are afraid they will forget that they have something if they can't see it. They tend to be more visual and want to be able to see their stuff at all times. For these individuals, out of sight is truly out of mind. Visual people tend to gravitate toward open shelving with clear, see-through containers and hanging systems in the garage. Convenient access for this type of person is to have as much as possible within arm's reach.

Other people find visual clutter unsettling or even downright disturbing and have a tendency to store items out of sight in cabinets and drawers. For these types of people, the less visible clutter the better. See-through storage containers are less important to this crowd than proper labeling. They are willing to go through more steps to retrieve something in order to maintain their visual sense of order. Knowing where to retrieve something when they need it is sufficient and they don't need to have everything within arm's reach.

You are wise to listen to your inner voice and select the storage options with which you feel most comfortable. If you don't, your system will be more difficult to maintain and have less chance of becoming a lasting one. A visual person who likes to see everything, yet has chosen a closed-door cabinet system or has put everything on shelves in boxes that are not see-through, is far more likely not to be able to find things or to be resistant to putting things away and keeping up with the system than a person who has acknowledged his or her personal preferences up front.

Assessing Storage Options

In addition to your storage style, many other factors play a role in determining what type of storage works best for your particular storage location and stored items. Here are some points to consider when choosing storage solutions:

- **The size and design of your garage**—A major factor in choosing a particular storage option is the size of your garage and its layout. If your garage is very small, you would be well advised to hang as much as possible on the walls to maximize your space and create loft storage by utilizing the upper portions of the walls and ceiling (this will be discussed later in this chapter). If you are lucky, your garage has lots of windows that will provide lots of natural light. However, this will limit the amount of hanging space you have available for rakes, shovels, and brooms. Although your preference might be to hang as much as possible, your available wall space could dictate otherwise.

- **The quantity of the groups of items you store**—Your storage system must be appropriate for the collections of items you'll be storing. If you have a small amount of camping equipment, for example, a labeled storage container on a shelf could work just fine. However, if you have an extensive amount of camping gear, you might want to devote an entire cabinet to it.

- **The size and dimensions of the items you store**—Beyond accommodating the collective size of your items, the storage system also needs to be appropriate for the size and dimensions of the items you store. Long-handled items, such as rakes and brooms, lend themselves to hanging storage, and many products are available for this purpose. Small nuts and bolts are easily stored in small drawers, compartmentalized containers, cans with lids, or jars.

- **Frequency of use**—Providing easy access to frequently used items is another important factor in choosing a suitable storage option. If you make frequent camping trips, you will want to store your camping equipment in a convenient, accessible location. However, if you go only once a year, loft storage would be quite suitable. And, of course, if you haven't gone in the past five years, you need to question why you are holding on to this equipment at all.

As you will quickly begin to see, there is no one right answer to the question of what's the best storage option for a particular item. Although there is often a more common, appropriate, or desirable approach to storing something, there is almost always more than one way to do it. Table 3.1 provides a general guide for some of the more commonly used methods of storage. Later in the chapter, you will be prepared to make some specific choices that will work best for you. In the table,

note Remember, there are many "right" ways to store any item. Storage options not indicated in Table 3.1 aren't unsuitable solutions—they simply are less common choices. Always use your imagination and choose a solution that works best for you.

I've marked my personal storage preferences with a bold **x**, but other methods are indicated that might work for you as well. If the **x** is followed by an asterisk (*), this indicates that you might want to seriously consider placing the item(s) in an appropriate container before you store them. The additional blank lines will allow you to write in items you have that are not included in this list. The later section, "Choosing Storage Methods That Work for You," includes a blank version of this chart in which you can mark your own preferences.

Table 3.1 Suitable Storage Options

Item Stored	Hang	Shelf	Drawer	Cabinet	Loft	Floor
Balls		x*				x*
Baseball bats	x					x*
Bicycles	x					x
Brooms/mops	x					x*
Buckets	x					x
Cable, wire, rope	x		x	x*		
Camping equipment		x*		x*	x*	
Canoe/kayak	x				x	
Car seat	x				x	
Chemicals		x		x		
Cleaning products		x		x		
Clothing	x		x			
Electrical supplies		x*	x	x*		
Extension cords	x		x	x*		
Fishing rods	x					x*
Folding chairs	x					x

Item Stored	Hang	Shelf	Drawer	Cabinet	Loft	Floor
Folding tables	X					X
Food items		X		X		
Garden hose	X					
Hand tools	X	X*	X	X*		
Holiday decorations		X*		X*	X*	
Items with handles	X		X			
Ladders	X					X
Lawn chairs	X				X	X
Lawn tools	X		X	X		
Luggage		X			X	
Lumber		X			X	
Paint cans		X		X		X
Paint supplies		X	X	X		
Patio furniture	X				X	X
Pesticides		X		X		
Plumbing supplies		X*	X	X*		
Power tools	X	X	X	X		
Skis	X				X	
Weed trimmer	X	X		X		
Wheelbarrow	X				X	

To do list

- ☐ Learn cost-effective ways to create hanging storage.
- ☐ Use specially designed hooks for easy hanging.
- ☐ Discover unconventional hanging storage techniques.
- ☐ Utilize ready-made wall-mounted hanging devices.
- ☐ Learn innovative ways to use pegboard hanging systems.

Hanging Things Up

Whether you are a visual person who likes to see everything or you are just trying to make the most efficient use of your limited space, it is hard to beat the functionality and versatility of a hanging system. As you can see in Table 3.1, hanging systems are commonly used for storing many of the items commonly found in the garage. From conventional pegboard, standalone hooks, and multi-item holders, to the gaining popularity of slatwall systems, which will be discussed in Chapter 4, there is a hanging system to match everyone's budget.

A slatwall system is a grooved panel or series of panels installed directly onto the garage wall. A wide variety of accessories (hooks, shelves, and baskets) are manufactured to fit into the slotted grooves that hold just about anything. More than likely, you have already seen them in clothing stores and other retail establishments, but only recently have they become prominent in higher-end garage systems as well.

tip Whether you have decided to hang your folding chairs or stack them upright on the floor, it can be a chore to keep them clean between each use. Consider putting a slipcover over them to keep them from getting dusty and having to clean them every time you use them. One easy way is to cut open the bottom of an old garment bag and slip it over the stacked chairs. You can also use a large plastic lawn-and-leaf bag for this purpose. Slipcovering is also an excellent way to keep luggage and other less frequently used items clean while they're stored. To protect your clothing, hang it in a cloth garment bag rather than a plastic one, so the clothes can breathe.

Things You'll Need

- ☐ Hammer and nails
- ☐ Cup hooks
- ☐ Bungee cords
- ☐ Furring strips
- ☐ Utility hooks and/or wall-mounted holders
- ☐ Pegboard and hooks

Simple, Inexpensive Hanging Storage Solutions

You don't have to break the bank to create a simple hanging storage system. Here are some economical ways to hang things in your garage:

- The most inexpensive way I know to hang any object from the wall is by hammering a nail into the stud and using the nail head as a hook. Most "hangable" items have a hole in their handle specifically for this purpose, so use large finishing nails with heads small enough to fit through the holes. If an object you want to hang has a solid wooden handle, drill a hole through it. If you find it difficult to drill a big enough hole for it to fit over the nail, insert a piece of string or cord through the hole, tie a knot, and hang the item up.

- Another easy way to hang something is to hammer two nails in half way, side by side, spaced far enough apart to accommodate the width of the handle. With the tip of the handle pointing downward, as shown in Figure 3.1, the nails will support the larger end of the object.

- In an unfinished garage, you can make good use of the exposed studs and slats by hanging things on nails or hooks attached to the fronts or sides of the studs themselves or from the support ledge between the studs, as shown in Figure 3.2. Another clever way to hang things from the support ledge between the studs is by using large screw-in cup hooks.

caution Be careful to hang sharp objects safely. Sharp objects such as hoes or rakes can harm you if you brush up against them or if they fall and strike you. This danger is increased when you hang these objects with the handle pointed down.

FIGURE 3.1

This is an economical way to hang shovels, brooms, and rakes.

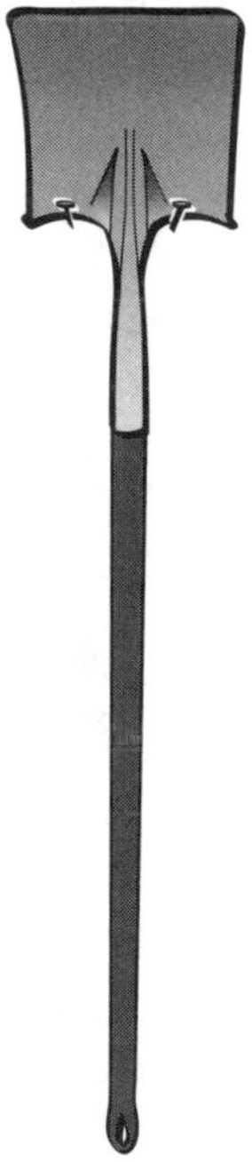

FIGURE 3.2

If your garage has exposed studs, you can store many items on hooks or shelves.

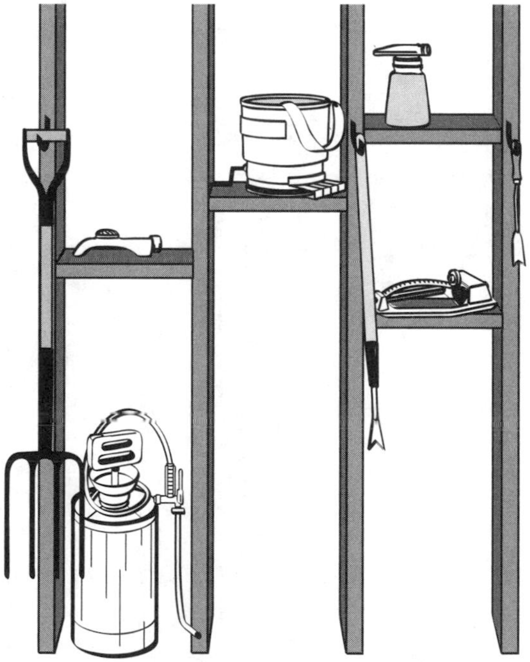

- Nailing clothes pins to a stud with finishing nails enables you to clip small items, such as goggles, to the stud, as shown in Figure 3.3.

FIGURE 3.3
Using clothes pins is another way to maximize storage space between exposed studs.

- If you are storing items between the studs, suspend bungee cords between two nails or nail small braces (1"×2" furring strips cut to the desired length) into the studs to hold the items in place, as shown in Figure 3.4. This is a great way to store long items such as rakes, skis, and lumber, keeping them out of the way and off the floor.

FIGURE 3.4
Adding support braces enables you to store items between exposed studs with no risk of them falling.

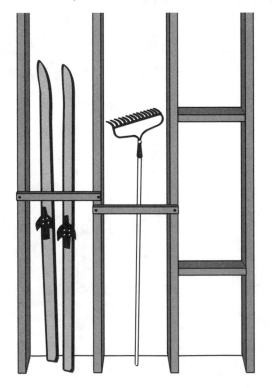

Hang It with a Hook

Many types and varieties of durable hooks are available at hardware and discount stores. These can be purchased individually or in assorted packs, as shown in Figure 3.5, to hang items large and small. Some are specifically designed to hold tools, whereas others are better suited to hold larger items such as ladders, brooms, and bicycles. The most common types are rubber coated to protect your items from getting scratched and damaged. The opposite end is threaded like a large screw. After pre-drilling the appropriately sized hole, simply screw the hook in to a stud, and it is ready to begin working for you.

FIGURE 3.5

The utility hooks in this multipack are designed to hang a wide variety of items.

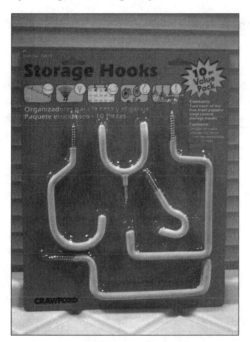

And trust me, ladder hooks (the largest hook in the package shown in Figure 3.5) aren't just for hanging ladders. It is amazing how something so inexpensive can have so many uses and be so versatile. By screwing ladder hooks in to ceiling joists, you can hang a multitude of large items on them, including bicycles, tires, fans, and lawn chairs, just to name a few.

Now that your creative juices are in overdrive in your quest to utilize every conceivable place on the garage ceiling and walls to hang things from, be cautious about hanging heavy items

caution

When using screw-in hooks to hang items, be sure to follow manufacturer recommendations for weight limitations. If you are in doubt, use a stronger hook than you think is necessary; better to err on the side of safety. This will ensure that the item won't fall and injure someone and damage your car or other nearby items.

from exposed pipes. These pipes are not designed to support much weight and can easily be damaged. However, by exercising a little common sense, these pipes can be utilized to hang lightweight items such as dust mops, dust pans, paint rollers, and empty buckets with the use of large S-hooks.

Hose hangers are a relic from the past that many have discarded in favor of portable hose reel carts. However, they are a great example of how, with a little ingenuity, we can find new uses for something old. By attaching a hose hanger to the wall of your garage, you can store heavy-duty extension cords on it—and even the flexible tubing from your shop vacuum—without damage.

Other Types of Wall Holders for Hanging Items

There are many different types of wall-mountable holders commercially available and designed to hang tools, cleaning items, sporting goods, and lawn and garden equipment in a variety of ways. The simplest types, as discussed earlier, involve a peg or hook from which you can hang the handle of the item. Wall-mounted holder grips are another option; you press the handle of items into the grips, which lock it into place. Another type of wall-mounted holder allows you to slide the handle through the holder's opening.

The holder shown in Figure 3.6 accommodates handles that have been outfitted to hang from pegs, as well as handles of varying sizes which fit in nonslip rubber-coated hooks.

One of the newest and more innovative types of holders is the Grook™ Tool Holder, shown in Figure 3.7, made by Casabella® products (www.casabella.com). It has non-slip rubber rings that accommodate handles in three ways: through the rings, between the rings, and on hooks in front of the rings. The Grook™ is durable and guaranteed not to rust. The smaller 11" size retails at around $20, whereas the larger length (17.25") retails at around $29.

Hanging on Pegboard: New Systems for an Old Favorite

Nothing seems to come close to matching the popularity, flexibility, convenience, and low cost of pegboard. Pegboard is a Masonite® sheet perforated by regularly spaced holes through which you can insert specially designed hooks, as shown in Figure 3.8.

FIGURE 3.6
This inexpensive wall-mounted holder is one of the many types available to hold brooms, mops, and shovels.

FIGURE 3.7
The durable aluminum and rubber Grook™ holder offers three options to maximize hanging storage and is guaranteed not to rust. (Photo courtesy of Casabella®.)

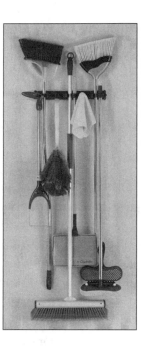

FIGURE 3.8
There are many specialty hooks you can use with pegboard.

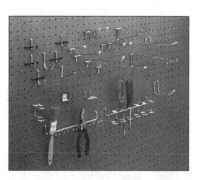

Pegboard is used to hang everything—tools above the workbench, sporting goods, extension cords, and large lawn and garden items. Hooks are available in a large variety of shapes and sizes, and many are designed specifically to hang certain types of items. They are sold in combination packages and can sometimes be bought individually.

Hooks are available in lengths up to a foot, and you can hang several lightweight tools on each one and conserve even more space. Although this is a great space-saving idea, there is a downside. To get to the fifth paint brush, you would need to remove the four in front of it first. Only you can decide if this minor inconvenience is worth the space savings.

Many people choose to leave pegboard unpainted in its natural state, but some prefer to paint it a light color, to help make hanging items easier to see. Some even go a step further by outlining the shape of the hung object with a dark marker to ensure that each item gets returned to its proper place.

HOW TO INSTALL PEGBOARD

If your garage doesn't already have pegboard on one or more walls, you can install it yourself. One of the easiest ways to install pegboard is in an unfinished garage. You simply nail the sheet of pegboard over the exposed studs and you are ready to go. If you are lucky enough to be in this situation, you can create an entire wall of hanging space in no time! However, don't overdo it. One 4'×8' sheet is ample for most people.

If you are going to put pegboard on top of finished garage walls, you will first need to install spacers on the wall to create a gap between the pegboard and the wall in order for the hooks to hang properly on it. The inch of space needed between the wall and the back of the pegboard is most easily attained by nailing 1"×2" furring strips to the wall at designated intervals.

One of the newest innovations in the world of pegboards is the Bunjipeg™, shown in Figure 3.9. Winner of the most outstanding product at the 2003 National Hardware Show in Chicago, the Bunjipeg™ can hold tools and items of virtually any size or shape firmly to the pegboard, with no custom metal hangers, hooks, or adaptors needed.

FIGURE 3.9

The Bunjipeg™ system provides a whole new way of hanging things on pegboard. (Photo courtesy of Bunjipeg™.)

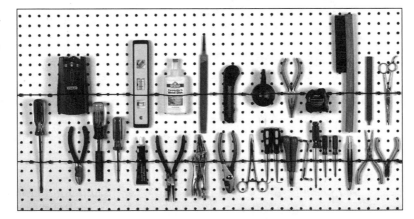

To set up the hanging system, you simply insert a forked peg over the elastic cord at one end of the pegboard, as shown in Figure 3.10, and continue this process in a straight line, skipping a couple holes between each peg to hold smaller items and skipping three or four holes to hold the larger ones. Slip the tools in behind the cord so they are held snugly in place. The pegs hold the elastic cord in place, and they are easy to move and rearrange as your needs change. The Bunjipeg™ system is especially great for tools with no ready-made holes for hanging or that common pegboard hooks won't accommodate.

FIGURE 3.10

The Bunjipeg™ system can be installed in a matter of minutes to provide a hanging storage solution with a wide range of flexibility. (Photo courtesy of www.bunjipeg.com.)

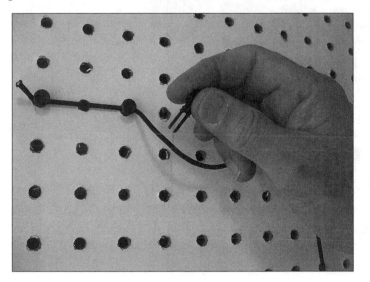

Currently, the Bunjipeg™ system is only available online at www.bunjipeg.com. Ten feet of the elastic cord can hold anywhere from 25 to 50 tools. A set of 24 pegs with 10' of cord sells for $9 and is enough to hold 50 tools. The best deal is a set of 40 pegs with 18' of cord, which is sold for $10 and holds up to 80 tools. The budget pack includes 100 pegs with 40' of cord for $20. Plans are in the works to offer the Bunjipeg™ system as a set with the pegboard included.

A new and innovative soft-sided product manufactured by Case Logic is a modular storage solution called Space Logic™, which is designed to hang from just about any-where—including pegboard! The tool and accessory organizer shown in Figure 3.11 has two easy-access sturdy shelves to store bulky items easily and two large tear-resistant mesh pockets below. The complete Space Logic™ system is available at Target, ShopKo, and Fred Meyer stores nationwide and online at www.stacksand-stacks.com. Prices range from $10 to $30 per component. You learn more about this system in Chapter 4.

FIGURE 3.11

This tool and accessory organizer installs in seconds and provides a unique and quick solution for garage storage. (Photo courtesy of Space Logic™.)

To do list

- ☐ Use shelves to your best advantage.
- ☐ Keep things organized on shelves.
- ☐ Use shelving in cabinets or closets.

Setting Up Shelving

There is little question that some portion of your garage storage system will require the use of shelving. Next to hanging, shelving is the next most popular and practical storage method. Open shelving is great for the storage of large, bulky items such as ice chests and smaller items alike. Also, open shelving makes it easy to see what you have. Because shelving can be used to store items in plain view, as well as in cabinets behind closed doors, it is an ideal solution for both visual and nonvisual storage preferences.

Although it is easy to find a shelving system for virtually any budget (as you learn in Chapter 4), you need to keep in mind these important considerations to make the best use of the shelving unit you ultimately select:

- Shelves should be deep enough to safely store items, yet not so deep that items will get hidden behind each other. For a garage, 16" depth is ideal for the storage of large items and 12" depth is ideal for smaller items.

- Adjustability is very important to maximize the use of space. Fixed shelving creates a lot of wasted space between the shelves.

- It is better to have more shelves and space them closer together so that you aren't tempted to stack things too high on a single shelf. Tall stacks of items can fall, and it is more difficult to find and organize things within such stacks.

- Store frequently used items on the shelves at waist height, where they're easiest to access; store the items you use less frequently on higher or lower shelving. Heavier things should be stored near the floor so if they do fall, they are far less likely to hurt anyone.

- Keep newer backup replacement items behind the older items on the shelf, similar to the way items are displayed in a grocery store. That way, you use the older things first.

- Ideally, shelves should be 6" to 1' off the floor to keep the items stored on them clean and dry. This also leaves the floor area for storage of bulky and heavy items such as shop vacuums and five-gallon containers.

- Enclosing the shelves within a cabinet or behind doors is a great help in keeping your items clean. One way to accomplish this is to build simple walls around your shelving units and create a closet enclosure with sliding doors.

To do list

- ❑ Shelving unit
- ❑ Shelf dividers
- ❑ Storage containers
- ❑ Container-labeling markers/tags
- ❑ Child-proof lock (where appropriate)

Using Dividers and Containers to Keep Your Shelves Organized

One of the major challenges in using any shelving system is keeping the shelves organized over time. Shelf dividers are a useful tool to slide on to the shelf and keep the items separated. However, nothing matches the usefulness of containers to store like items together and keep the items on your shelves neat. Square storage containers with lids work well because they stack neatly and come in a wide range of sizes. They can hold anything from household extension cords to painting, plumbing, and electrical supplies, as shown in Figure 3.12. As long as the containers are properly labeled, you will have no problem finding what you are looking for. You might consider labeling the shelves themselves if they contain only one type of item.

FIGURE 3.12
Plumbing and electrical supplies are neatly sorted and stored in these labeled containers.

Most households already have many types of containers that also work well to keep your shelves in good order. Large plastic crates work well to store all kinds of things, as do plastic dish tubs, margarine bowls, and yogurt containers. Don't throw away your old food storage containers if they become stained or you lose the lid. The garage is the perfect place to utilize them and give them new life.

Cabinetry with Shelves

One of the key advantages to using cabinets outfitted with adjustable shelves is that things can be stored out of sight. Also, because stored items are not directly exposed to airborne dust and dirt, they will stay much cleaner. If you are storing food items that won't fit in your kitchen pantry or that you have bought in bulk, a closed cabinet is preferable to open shelving.

Safety is another important advantage of storing potentially harmful and lethal substances in cabinets that can't be opened by young children. Cabinets equipped with a lock are the ideal place for toxic chemicals, mineral spirits, oils, lubricants, garden fertilizers and fungicides, and spray paint. If the cabinet you already own did not come with a locking mechanism, you should purchase and install a childproof lock.

Storing in Drawers

Drawers come in all shapes and sizes and are suitable for storing a wide variety of things—plumbing and electrical supplies, hand tools, and even smaller items such as nuts and bolts. Drawer units can sit on the floor and smaller units can be placed on top of your workbench or shelves. They can be made of wood, metal, or plastic, and many of the smaller table-top units are transparent so you can see what is inside.

There are some key advantages to storing things in drawers. Because they are usually smaller than a shelf and easily compartmentalized, drawers can be ideal for storing like items together, such as tools (as shown in Figure 3.13), supplies, crafts, or anything that could be stored in an individual plastic storage box. Drawers provide easy access and keep stored items clean and less susceptible to infestation by insects and rodents than when items are hanging or sitting on shelves.

FIGURE 3.13

A drawer is the perfect place to store hand tools, such as this complete set of wrenches.

Depending on the size of the drawer and the size of the items being stored in it, some stored items will need to be containerized first and others will not. If the drawers are small, you can designate and label each drawer with the type of item being stored in it. If the drawer is larger and the items you are storing in it are small, you will want to use appropriately sized and labeled plastic containers to keep the contents from becoming mixed and creating a junk drawer. It is also important to be careful not to overload the drawer, because this will make it heavy to open and the objects within it difficult to find.

Another way to separate items in a drawer is to partition it with plastic drawer dividers, similar to those one would use in a kitchen utensil drawer. Other commonly used items can assist with this task, such as cutlery and ice cube trays, cardboard boxes, and cookie tins.

Things You'll Need

- ☐ Drawer unit (if appropriate)
- ☐ Drawer dividers (if desired)
- ☐ Storage containers

Storing on the Floor... or Not

The garage floor often becomes the "catchall" storage location by default and the primary reason for this is that adequate storage systems that are appropriate and accessible have not been created. The garage floor is considered to be extremely valuable real estate, especially if you plan to park your cars there. Over time, a few objects here and there will eventually become a huge pile of clutter and edge your automobiles right out of the garage.

One of my cardinal rules is to get things off the floor whenever possible. This will maximize your space and your garage will seem less cluttered and look more spacious. There are many practical reasons for not wanting to store things on the floor. They become harder to find, and unless your garage is a climate-controlled room, things can get wet, dirty, or more easily come into contact with insects and rodents.

However, let me also be clear in saying that there are certainly legitimate reasons for storing items on the floor. Where else would you store a lawnmower, snow blower, generator, power washer, and other large, bulky, and heavy items, unless you also have the luxury of a shed? (You learn more about shed storage in Chapter 5, "Analyzing Alternative Storage Solutions.") Of course, many cabinets are designed to be placed on the floor, but be careful about using cabinets made from wood or particle board on a floor that is prone to flooding. My recommendation is that you carefully consider alternative options before deciding on the floor as a final storage place. If nowhere else makes sense, the floor could very well be an appropriate option for you to consider.

PROTECT ITEMS YOU STORE ON THE FLOOR

No matter how often I advise people not to store valuable and important items in the garage—and especially on the floor—they are still going to do it. If you are going to store on the floor, be sure you take every precaution to protect your items from damage. If your floor has a tendency to flood, raise things off the floor on wooden pallets or on elevated plywood sheets placed on bricks. Plastic or metal trash cans are inexpensive and ideal storage containers for items with long handles, balls, rags, and other items you decide to store on the floor. The trash can protects stored items from getting

broken or wet. If you live in an area plagued with roaches, mice, and other vermin, you can use boric acid to cut down on the roach population as well as high-frequency plug-in bug and rodent deterrents.

Do not store bags of pet food on the floor because they can easily become wet and infested with insects or penetrated by rodents. Many types of air-tight plastic pet food storage bins are available, such as those shown here, that keep the food fresh and unwanted visitors out. Some of these containers sit on shelves or the floor, whereas others mount on the wall. They are all available in assorted stackable sizes in pet stores and discount stores everywhere.

To do list

☐ Analyze storage options on the ceiling and upper walls.

☐ Consider loft and rafter storage to maximize space.

☐ Create loft storage in many ways.

☐ Lift large, heavy items out of the way.

Using the Ceiling to Create More Storage

Frequently in this chapter I've talked about the importance of maximizing the usage of your garage walls and minimizing storage on the floor. One good way to make the most of your garage storage space is by using the rafters or suspending loft storage from the ceiling. Many people overlook this huge expanse of space, which can be ideal for seasonal storage and things that are not accessed on a frequent basis.

Both loft and rafter storage are ideal for keeping less frequently used items out of the way. Rafter storage is especially useful to store items such as bed frames, fishing poles, skis, and other long items that can be suspended between the rafters themselves. It is also a great place to store pieces of lumber. However, make sure you label the end with the length so you don't have to keep measuring the pieces over and over. By installing full sheets of 3/4" plywood across the tops of the rafters, you can create instant makeshift attic storage that's easily accessible and can accommodate smaller items. Suspended loft storage can be ideal for storing even larger items such as furniture, suitcases, camping gear, and off-season items such as holiday decorations and patio furniture.

To keep the stored items clean, cover them with plastic tarps or old sheets if they need to breathe. Use jumbo heavy-duty lawn bags for luggage, fans, and other large items. Kitchen trash bags work well to protect smaller items such as sleeping bags and smaller suitcases.

Things You'll Need

- ❏ Loft storage system (if appropriate)
- ❏ Three-quarter-inch plywood sheets
- ❏ Plastic tarps and jumbo heavy-duty lawn bags

Installing Your Own Loft Storage

Loft storage is most commonly installed in the unused area above the garage door and can significantly increase your overall storage capacity. The only drawback is that this area can only be accessed when the garage door is down, and it's difficult to reach when the garage door is up. However, this is a small price to pay for the versatility it provides and the storage space you will gain.

One of the least expensive ways to create loft storage is by inserting several screw-in hooks from studs in the ceiling and suspending equal lengths of chain from them. Then, by attaching a piece of plywood to the ends of the chains with S-hooks, you will create overhead storage that can be used for all kinds of things. Use heavy-gauge hooks and chain and be careful not to store items up there that are extremely heavy. If you are in doubt, seek the assistance of a professional carpenter. In Figure 3.14, you see how one homeowner designed loft storage by using heavy-duty brackets and scrap lumber to store plastic boxes and get them out of the way.

FIGURE 3.14

With a few brackets and some lumber, you can quickly create loft storage like this.

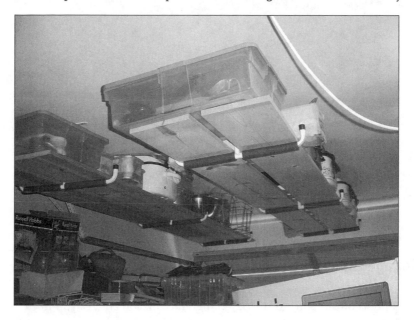

Another option to create loft storage quickly over the garage door is to use an adjustable shelving system, such as one manufactured by Elfa® or Schulte® (you learn more about these systems in "Creating a Storage System for Less than $500," in Chapter 4). In such a system, a track or rail is attached at the top of the wall near the ceiling, and hardware to which brackets are attached is hung from the rail. The ventilated wire shelving is available in 12", 16", and 20" depths and snaps onto the standards with brackets wherever you want.

The Hy-Loft® storage system (www.hyloft.com) shown in Figure 3.15 is a great option for the quick-and-easy addition of suspended loft storage in your garage, as well as other rooms of your home. These ventilated shelves are supported with adjustable brackets suspended from the ceiling or can be mounted on the wall with brackets. They are made of durable steel with a scratch-resistant finish and come in three major sizes with a lifetime warranty. This product is versatile enough to hold anything from large, bulky items to heavy boxes of archived files with a weight load capacity of up to 250 pounds and over 30 cubic feet of storage capacity. What's more, accessory baskets can be suspended from the loft. Hy-Loft® systems are available for less than $75 at major home improvement stores as well as in discount stores.

FIGURE 3.15
Hy-Loft® helps you create space in places you never thought of using. (Photo courtesy of Hy-Loft®.)

Loft-It® Storage Lift System

Have you ever asked yourself how you are going to park your cars in the garage and still accommodate all the other large motorized vehicles you need to store? What does a person do if he or she has a riding lawnmower or motorcycle and wants to get it out of the way during the winter months when it is not being used? Or what does that person do to store a snow blower and snowmobile during the summer? Aside from getting an outdoor shed or having a three-car garage, there haven't been many options until now.

One of the newer innovations on the market to deal with this problem is the Loft-It® Storage Lift System (www.loft-it.com). The mechanical lift shown in Figure 3.16 can raise 1,000 pounds up to 6' off the ground on its 4'×8' platform. You must insert a key into the control box to raise or lower the platform, which ensures safe and smooth operation. The system comes with do-it-yourself installation instructions, or it can be installed by a hired contractor. With a one-year warranty and a cost of approximately $2,000 installed, your Loft-It® Storage Lift System can store anything from bicycles to a riding mower, getting them up and out of the way until you need them.

With the Loft-It® Storage Lift System, motorcycles and other large items are hoisted out of your way with ease. (Photo courtesy of Loft-It®.)

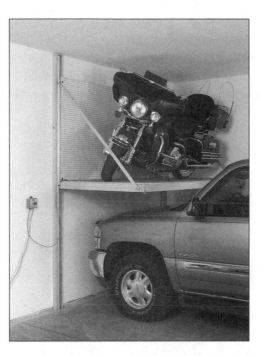

Choosing Storage Methods That Work for You

Now that you understand the basic types of storage options available and why one method might be preferable to another for a particular item, it is time to choose the storage methods that are right for you and will work best in your garage to store your stuff. By determining this now, you will be better prepared to analyze the storage systems available in Chapter 4 and have a clearer idea of which products or system will best meet your requirements. You might just discover that you already have everything you need in your garage or home.

Table 3.2 contains a list of items typically stored in the garage. Columns are provided for you to indicate the method of storage you want to use for those items. Place an "X" in the appropriate column that corresponds to the way you intend to store a particular item in your garage. Refer to the garage plan you created in Chapter 1 to help you.

Do not worry about making the "wrong" decision. Remember, I told you earlier that there is no right or wrong decision. You simply need to create a system that works best for you. The storage method you choose for a particular item is not cast in stone at this point, but this process will help you assess your storage system requirements before you review the storage systems showcased in the next chapter.

Feel free to flip back to Table 3.1 for quick reference if you are having trouble deciding. Use the blank lines at the bottom to write in additional kinds of items you have that are not included in the table. You will use this table as your guide in determining the type of storage system you need. After you have decided how you will store each item, determine whether you already have the system to store the item or will need to buy it.

Table 3.2   Selecting Your Storage Method

Item Stored	Hang	Shelf	Drawer	Cabinet	Loft	Floor	Have	Need
Balls								
Baseball bats								
Bicycles								
Brooms/mops								
Buckets								
Cable, wire, rope								
Camping equipment								
Canoe/kayak								
Car seat								
Chemicals								
Cleaning products								
Clothing								
Electrical supplies								
Extension cords								
Fishing rods								
Folding chairs								
Folding tables								
Food items								
Garden hose								
Hand tools								
Holiday decorations								
Items with handles								
Ladders								
Lawn chairs								
Lawn tools								

Item Stored	Hang	Shelf	Drawer	Cabinet	Loft	Floor	Have	Need
Luggage								
Lumber								
Paint cans								
Paint supplies								
Patio furniture								
Pesticides								
Plumbing supplies								
Power tools								
Skis								
Weed trimmer								
Wheelbarrow								

Summary

Now that you have a clear understanding of the types of storage methods available and which ones will work best for the items you have to store in your garage, you are ready to select your storage system. Don't worry. This does not mean you need to be prepared to spend an inordinate amount of money to get what you need. In the next chapter, you will learn how to utilize things you already own but never thought of using in this way. Also, if you do decide to upgrade or purchase a new component or two—or an entire new system—you will find a multitude of options for doing so, in all price ranges.

Selecting Storage Systems

In the last chapter, you learned the appropriate methods for storing various items and made some choices regarding how you will store what you have in your garage. You began to analyze your current system and made some decisions about systems you already have that are working and what you might need to purchase. If your garage is already outfitted with shelves, cabinets, and drawer systems that are appropriate for what you are storing and work reasonably well, you might just need to tweak your current storage system by assigning a more appropriate home for your things and organizing them better.

In this chapter, you will take a closer look at the systems you are currently using and decide whether you want to make some changes, add to these systems, or start off by buying an entire new system. You will learn how your current garage setup stacks up to what is available and whether you need to consider purchasing additional storage systems such as those showcased in this chapter.

To do list

❑ Determine what current storage is working for you (and what isn't).

❑ Consider items you are no longer using that could be used for storage.

Using What You Already Have

As previously mentioned, chances are you already have some good organizing systems in place and don't need to start from scratch. If you're satisfied with your existing storage systems, there is no need to change them. Over the years, I have seen some of the most antiquated and dilapidated systems work just fine in keeping people's garages organized.

Before deciding to buy additional systems to organize your garage, look around the house and ask yourself if you have furniture you are no longer using or have thought of replacing that you could use in your garage. Some of these items might have already been relegated to the garage; that dresser, buffet, or cabinet no longer served a function inside the house, yet was too good to give away or get rid of, so out to the garage it went. Often, these kinds of items make some of the best and more original garage storage systems, not to mention all the fond memories they bring back when you see them.

Here are just a few of the items you might no longer be using and are just sitting around your house that could be given a whole new life in the garage:

- Chests of drawers or dressers
- Kitchen islands
- Bookcases
- Baby furniture
- Entertainment centers
- Toy chests
- Wall units
- Rolling carts
- Shelving units
- TV carts
- Kitchen cabinets
- Filing cabinets
- Desks
- Closet organizers

I can already hear some of you saying, "I paid a lot of money for some of this stuff and it is too good to use out in the garage." Be practical and think of it this way: These items have served you well for many years and will probably provide more value to you in your garage than the money you might get if you sold any of them as second-hand furniture or in a garage sale.

Utilizing kitchen cabinets and countertops, as shown in Figure 4.1, is one of the best examples of recycling something that has outlived its original use and giving it a whole new life in the garage. By far, this is one of my favorite ways to economically create a complete garage storage system. If you plan to remodel your kitchen or know someone who is, install these old kitchen cabinets and countertops in your garage. If you have a brand new kitchen, consider visiting Habitat for Humanity or contacting a kitchen cabinet installer because some will make old cabinets available for a price you can't afford to pass up. If you are willing to spend the time scouting, you can sometimes find cabinets on clearance at a home improvement center that were returned because they were the wrong size or had scratches.

FIGURE 4.1

Create a complete garage storage solution with your old kitchen cabinets.

The kitchen isn't the only place in your home with cabinets that will work well to create your dream garage at a fraction of the price of buying something new. The wall cabinets shown in Figure 4.2 were salvaged from a family room renovation and provide an entire wall of concealed storage.

FIGURE 4.2
These old family room cabinets provide floor-to-ceiling storage to conceal a wide variety of items.

THE VERSATILITY OF FILING CABINETS

There are many ways in which you can use an old filing cabinet. Of course, you can use it to archive financial files, such as prior years' receipts and tax returns, but it will also hold owner's manuals and other reference items, and so much more. By using hanging files, you can easily store the various grits of sandpaper you can never find when you need them or the many sewing patterns you have collected over the years. If you think of the cabinet as oversized drawers, this expands the range of possibilities to store electronic and computer cables, wires, cords, and connectors, as well as little cans of paint and stain. You can devote an entire drawer to a type of item, such as light bulbs, or a particular hobby or craft. Another great idea is to assign each drawer to a family member to store his or her own personal sporting goods, such as bike helmet, roller blade pads, balls, or anything that only that person uses.

To do list

- ☐ Determine what storage containers, cabinets, and so on, you need.
- ☐ Set a budget for a storage system.
- ☐ Determine what you will buy now or defer to later.
- ☐ Choose between wall-mounted and freestanding system components.
- ☐ Choose between open and closed shelving.

Making Basic Decisions About Your Storage System

You have made up your mind, and based on your needs assessment in the last chapter, you know you are going to have to purchase something, but what? Because there are so many choices out there, how can you be sure you are buying the right thing? The good news here is that you have an endless list of possibilities to choose from, and as long as you have determined the type of system or components you need, there are many ways to achieve the same end result.

Things You'll Need

- ☐ Table 3.2 from the previous chapter
- ☐ Your garage plan from Chapter 1, "Where Do I Begin?"
- ☐ Pen and paper

Using your garage plan from Chapter 1 and Table 3.2 from Chapter 3, "Reviewing Storage Options," review the storage centers you plan to create and the storage methods you plan to use within each area. To house and containerize your items, you might choose to use things you already have, as previously discussed in this chapter, or you might choose to purchase a few new products or a completely new system. Once you know what type of storage you need, you will be much better able to decide which of the storage systems discussed later in this chapter will best meet your needs. You have many things to consider before deciding which garage system is right for you. One of the most obvious considerations is your budget. Others are functionality and adjustability, so as your needs change over time, your system can change with them.

Determine Your Budget

Even if you decide you need to purchase additional storage systems, the good news is that you don't need to spend a lot of money to have an organized garage. You can organize your garage on a shoe-string budget or spend as much as you want—that's up to you. By using your imagination, you can put things to work you already have around the house or in the garage that are just taking up space, or you can buy storage units at somebody else's garage sale. I believe that the garage is one area where function over form is paramount. Your budget and imagination will determine your options.

If you have made up your mind that you won't settle for anything less than a new system, you'll find plenty of options available in all price ranges. Fortunately, you don't have to purchase the entire system all at once; you can buy what you need now and acquire other components over time. At this point, the important thing is for you to determine how much you are willing to spend now or over time on a new storage system or components to complement what you already have.

Once you have decided how much you are comfortable spending, you will find it much easier to use this book to help you decide what to buy. The storage systems highlighted in this chapter are divided into three main price categories: less than $500 (economical), from $500 to $1,000 (mid-range) and more than $1,000 (high end). Of course, some of the systems mentioned in each price range can easily end up costing more, depending on how many components you purchase, so these price ranges should be viewed as general guidelines.

Determine the Type of Storage System You Want

There are basically two types of garage storage systems: freestanding or wall-mounted. The freestanding system sits on the floor, whereas the wall-mounted system mounts on the wall. Although either type works well, both have their advantages and disadvantages.

Wall-mounted systems are ideal because they keep items off the floor, and the space might otherwise be wasted. With these systems, things are more visible, and if your garage is prone to flooding, your stored items are stashed safely above the flooded area. Although they tend to be more expensive, wall-mounted systems are generally durable and built to provide you with many years of service.

Many of the more inexpensive types of garage systems are freestanding systems. Because these systems sit on the garage floor, they are not the better choice if your garage has a tendency to flood. If the systems are made out of particle board or wood, they will warp and swell in damp conditions. However, even in lower-priced systems of this type, many are made of durable, heavy-weight molded plastic resin, which makes them impervious to water. Some of the higher-priced options have wheels, which automatically raise them several inches off the floor. Therefore, don't rule out freestanding systems altogether if you need storage in a damp garage. Some of the more expensive systems of this type have locking caster wheels, which allow you to move the entire unit and lock it in place.

Within either type of storage system, you can choose between open and closed shelving. This simply means that you will need to determine whether you want to store things out in the open on exposed shelving or whether you prefer cabinets with doors that close to conceal the shelving inside. As discussed in Chapter 3, this choice depends in part on your personal storage preferences and tolerance for visual clutter.

Items stored on open shelves can be easily seen and located. On the other hand, two of the greatest advantages for storing items in closed cabinets is that they will stay cleaner and can be locked away for increased safety.

Creating a Storage System for Less Than $500

You will be glad to know that this is the one price range with the widest variety of choices. Whether you are shopping at a large home improvement center or a discount superstore, I guarantee you will be able to find storage solutions that meet your needs, but won't break the bank. There are so many choices, your problem will not be finding a suitable product, but narrowing your choices down and selecting the one you like the best.

As a matter of fact, because of the unlimited assortment of storage options available in this price range, I had the same problem in deciding which ones to include in this book. My challenge was not in finding the products to showcase, but narrowing down the choices so this book would not end up being two or three times its current size. In order for a product to be featured in this section, it had to meet one of the following criteria:

- I have used the product personally or installed it for a client.
- I have been told by others that the product is great.
- I have reasonable familiarity with the particular product or other products made by that manufacturer.

I tried to include more of the newer, unique storage solutions and ones you might not have heard of to give you a broader range of options to choose from.

Things You'll Need

- ☐ The list of stored items and storage preferences from Table 3.2 in the previous chapter
- ☐ A list of existing storage components you would like to replace with new ones

Shelving Options

There are as many different sizes and styles of shelving systems as there are things to put on them. Some systems mount to the wall; others are floor-supported free-standing units. They are made of every type of material imaginable: wood, particle board, heavy-duty plastic resin, aluminum, steel, and any combination thereof. Even if you are not handy, you can snap a system together or build one "in no time."

Although you definitely do not have to spend a lot of money to get the shelving you need, you must keep some important points in mind before you buy so you can make a wise decision. This way, you won't have to replace the shelving in a couple years. This is one instance where it is well worth investing just a few dollars more to get something sturdy that will last. I have lost track of how many rusted, bent, and wobbly aluminum shelving units I have seen headed for the landfill over the years. Although they certainly have their place, know what you will be storing on them and be sure they are durable enough to support the anticipated weight.

Some manufacturers list the maximum weight their products will support and others don't. Just remember that it doesn't take much for the weight on these shelves to add up and quickly exceed the recommended weight limit.

Here are the major questions you need to answer in order to make a smart purchase for both floor-supported freestanding shelving units and wall-mounted shelving units:

- Is the shelving sturdy and stable?

  It is just as important for a shelving unit to be steady when it is empty, as when it is fully loaded. If the floor is uneven or the unit is wobbly, the whole thing can tip over, damaging the stored goods and harming anyone standing in its path. If you have any doubts, be sure to attach a freestanding shelving unit to the wall studs with bolts or brackets.

- Is the construction durable, and how much weight can the shelves hold?

  Shelves have the tendency to warp and sag over time, so know how much weight they can accommodate before you buy. Be sure to adhere to the weight limit recommendations of the manufacturer. Wall-supported systems offer the flexibility to install additional brackets if you know you will be storing extra-heavy items on the shelves.

- Is the shelving water resistant and rustproof?

If your garage is not waterproof, you should consider plastic or rust-resistant materials for floor-supported shelving units. Particle board and aluminum products should be avoided, unless you plan to raise them 6 inches off the floor with bricks or waterproof risers. This is less of a consideration for wall-supported shelving units.

- Are the shelves adjustable?

As you learned in Chapter 3, this is an important consideration, especially if your space is limited. Much valuable space is often lost between shelves that are spaced too far apart. With adjustable shelving, you can almost double the amount you can store in the same space.

- Is the shelving easy to assemble or install?

Depending on your level of handiness, be sure you or someone you know will be able to assemble or install the shelving. Having to hire someone to do this for you might easily surpass the cost of the shelving itself.

- Is the system easy to keep clean?

No matter which system you choose, it's going to get dirty out in the garage— there is no question about that. Wipeable materials such as plastic, aluminum, and steel are going to be much easier to keep clean than wood or particle board. Ventilated shelving is an excellent choice because it allows air to circulate more freely. Because it is not solid like wood, it doesn't trap the dirt.

Consider purchasing a shelving unit system as tall as the height of your garage wall will accommodate. For added safety, be sure to attach freestanding units to the wall. You can store seasonal decorations and other things you don't use often on the top shelves, and heavy items on the lowest shelves.

Remember the makeshift shelving people used to build in college with concrete blocks and planks of wood? If you are on a tight budget, this can be a quick and easy way to instantly create some of the shelving you need. However, unless you already have these materials lying around, it will probably be more economical to buy something ready-made and save yourself a lot of time and effort.

Freestanding Shelving

Although freestanding shelving units are made by several manufacturers and sold at home improvement outlets everywhere, one of the sturdiest, most economical, and versatile freestanding shelving systems is the Work Force™ unit, shown in Figure 4.3. Made of heavy-gauge steel and totally adjustable particle board shelves, this shelving system will hold up to 5,000 pounds and is available in heights up to 6' and widths of 4'. With only a rubber mallet needed for assembly, this unit can be configured in any number of ways and is available at major home improvement stores and discount stores everywhere.

FIGURE 4.3

This freestanding five-shelf unit is versatile and unsurpassed for strength and durability.

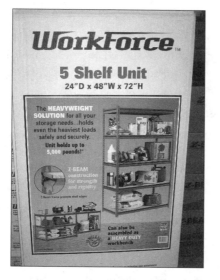

Other popular freestanding favorites are Metro® and InterMetro® ventilated shelving, shown in Figure 4.4. Available in black, silver, or white, each of these fully adjustable shelves can hold anywhere from 300 to 500 pounds. A starter system costs around $100 and comes with four shelves 48" long and 18" deep to build a unit 6' high. Additional shelves can be purchased individually, as well as sliding drawers and storage baskets that hook on the side. Assembly is easy and requires only a mallet. An added benefit to these shelving units is that casters can be purchased and installed if you want a portable shelving unit.

If you are looking for some freestanding shelving but prefer the heavy-duty molded resin type, few systems can beat the durability and dependability of Rubbermaid® products. Available at discount stores and home improvement centers nationwide, the five-shelf utility unit shown in Figure 4.5 is not only sturdy, but it resists moisture and will not warp, crack, rust, or rot. Each shelf holds up to 180 pounds, and the unit snaps together in minutes with no tools!

FIGURE 4.4

With a choice of three colors and easy adjustability, InterMetro® shelving is a stylish storage solution. (Photo courtesy of www.organize-everything.com.)

FIGURE 4.5

Assembly is a breeze for this molded resin shelving unit that won't warp, crack, or rust. (Photo courtesy of Rubbermaid®.)

And for those of you who want to maximize every square inch of space, Rubbermaid® makes a corner four-shelf unit that holds up to 720 or 180 pounds per adjustable shelf. Both units retail for less than $50.

The distinctive Box Warehouse shown in Figure 4.6 holds up to 12 storage boxes, ranging in size from 15 to 35 gallons. Your storage bins will easily slide in and out of this unique system designed to hold up to 1,200 pounds! The unit is easily assembled with a screwdriver and can be mounted to the wall for maximum stability. At just under 6' wide and 6' high, this space saver is available from Stacks and Stacks (www.stacksandstacks.com) for less than $160.

FIGURE 4.6

Store up to 12 containers in the unique Box Warehouse. (Photo courtesy of Stacks and Stacks.)

Wall-Mounted Shelving

Three of the more popular wall-mounted ventilated shelving systems are the Elfa®, Schulte®, and ClosetMaid® brands. Although each brand differs slightly in design and price, all of them offer a basic, affordable and easy-to-install garage shelving solution for less than $500. Of course, you can spend double that amount, depending on how much shelving and accessories your storage needs require.

One of the key advantages of these systems is their flexibility; the shelves are fully adjustable, so you can change their configuration as your needs change. The only portion of the system that actually attaches to your wall is the hanging rail itself. Standards are suspended from the hanging rail or track, and shelving brackets attach to the standards. The shelves simply snap into place on the brackets. You can create up to 50 linear feet of shelving in less than an hour.

The Elfa® system shown in Figure 4.7 is available through The Container Store® (www.thecontainerstore.com) in white or platinum, and all the materials have a 10-year warranty. The store's personnel offer free design and planning services, or you can design your garage online and pick it up at the store or have it shipped directly to you. The staff will cut all tracks, standards, and shelving to the lengths you require, eliminating the need for costly additional tools for installation. Of course, if you choose not to install the product yourself, you can hire a professional organizer or handyman to do so.

FIGURE 4.7

This basic Elfa® starter system is available in white and platinum. (Photo courtesy of The Container Store®.)

Schulte® products are available through Organized Living® stores (www.organizedliving.com) as well as dealers nationwide. To order online or to find a dealer in your area, visit the Schulte® website at www.schultestorage.com. The ClosetMaid® system shown in Figure 4.8 (www.closetmaid.com) is available at home improvement centers nationwide.

FIGURE 4.8

The MaxLoad system by ClosetMaid® is an affordable option for the budget-minded. (Photo courtesy of ClosetMaid®.)

One of the newest entrants to the wall-mounted shelving market is Rubbermaid's FastTrack® system, shown in Figure 4.9. One thing that differentiates this system from others of this type is that it includes a snazzy snap-on PVC cover. The rail of this system attaches to the wall studs, and the system offers both laminate and wire shelving options, which can be cut to any length. Over a dozen accessories and hooks have been specially designed to mount directly to the wall or snap on to the rail cover gripper and lock in place, which is another unique feature of this system. Each hook holds up to 50 pounds, has a protective coating, and can be repositioned in seconds. Currently available at Menard's and Bed Bath & Beyond, this system is not only easy to design, but easy to install. Best of all, you can outfit an entire wall for around $250.

Cabinet Solutions

Just as with the shelving options discussed in the last section, there are as many different sizes and styles of garage cabinetry as there are things to put in them. As noted earlier, cabinets help to keep stored items clean and create a safer garage environment for the entire family because you can store pesticides and harmful chemicals behind locked doors.

Some cabinets mount to the wall, and others are floor-supported freestanding units, with some sporting lockable wheels. You will be able to find cabinets made of every type of material imaginable: wood, particle board, heavy-duty plastic resin, aluminum, steel, and any combination thereof. There are many affordable options within each type, and most of them are easy to assemble and are quite durable and moisture resistant.

Wood and Laminate Cabinets

There are many low-cost cabinet options constructed of particle board covered with white or gray laminate; these units are easily assembled and very affordable. Virtually every home improvement retailer offers their own brand. These cabinets are available in all shapes and sizes and can be easily configured to meet your exact storage requirements. With most components selling for less than $100, these cabinets are both versatile and affordable.

O'Sullivan's Coleman® Renegade™, shown in Figure 4.10, is a versatile, tall, heavy-duty utility cabinet with two adjustable interior shelves. It stands a little over 6' high, and has a depth of almost 20". This cabinet is not equipped with a lock, but you can easily add one. This product retails for around $100 and can be found at Target stores or at numerous online retailers, including www.racksandstands.com.

FIGURE 4.10
FIGURE 4.10
The Coleman®
Renegade™ is a spa-
cious storage cabinet
designed to hold a
multitude of things.
(Photo courtesy of
O'Sullivan Furniture.)

Molded Plastic Resin Systems

Two great options in the molded resin line of products are the Rubbermaid® series, shown in Figure 4.11, and the Black & Decker® Space Rite® series. These cabinets are lockable and made of high-impact-resistant resin with adjustable shelves. They resist moisture and will not warp, crack, rust, or rot. Both companies manufacture utility cabinets that are 6' tall and base cabinets about 3' tall, available at home improvement stores and discount superstores nationwide. You are unlikely to exceed the weight capacities of over 600 pounds for the utility cabinets and 300 pounds for the base cabinets. One of my favorites in this series to maximize every bit of space is the Rubbermaid® stackable corner cabinet, shown in Figure 4.12.

FIGURE 4.11
The Rubbermaid®
system is versatile
and boasts one of the
highest weight
capacities of any
molded plastic sys-
tem. (Photo courtesy
of Rubbermaid®.)

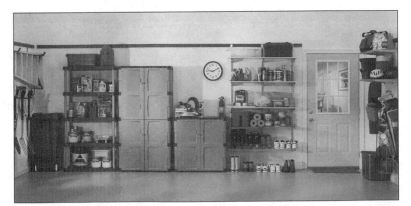

FIGURE 4.12
This Rubbermaid® stackable corner cabinet includes an adjustable shelf. (Photo courtesy of Rubbermaid®.)

Wall-Hanging Systems

If you are looking for an economical and versatile wall-hanging system, you might want to consider the unique Storage Track poly pegboard system shown in Figure 4.13. This system is easy to install and includes a set of slotted vinyl tracks that accommodate shelves and other accessories. The system is available in three sizes to work in all types of spaces; each size comes in a width of 48". The Value Kit, which is the smallest of the three, is priced at less than $75 and stands 17" tall. The Super Kit stands 30" tall and is priced around $90, and the Jumbo Kit is 48" tall and retails for less than $120. These systems are manufactured in Canada and distributed through dealers, which can be found at www.homeorganizers.ca.

At the 2004 National Hardware Show in Las Vegas, Case Logic launched the first line of soft-sided modular storage products for the garage and other hard-to-organize areas, called Space Logic™. Shown in Figure 4.14, these durable yet lightweight products have see-through and tear-resistant mesh storage pockets. You can mount these storage units with their heavy-duty reinforced mounting brackets on almost any finished or unfinished wall or surface, including pegboard, or you can hang them from metal, wood, or plastic shelving units. They are so functional and simply designed, with no sharp edges or hard surfaces, that they can be used to maximize storage space anywhere and hold just about anything. By using just one or any combination of the products in the series, you can organize sporting goods, tools, lawn and garden equipment, or paint and automotive supplies "in no time." Space Logic™ products are available at Target, ShopKo, and Fred Meyer stores nationwide and online at www.stacksandstacks.com, with a price ranging from $10 to $30 per item. These products are already catching on to satisfy a wide variety of garage storage needs.

FIGURE 4.13

This pegboard system includes a vinyl track for shelves and other accessories. (Photo courtesy of www. homeorganizers.ca.)

FIGURE 4.14

These soft-sided Space Logic™ modular storage products can satisfy a wide variety of garage storage needs. (Photo courtesy of Case Logic.)

The Schulte® grid system shown in Figure 4.15 is composed of heavy-gauge epoxy-coated steel grids that come in 2'×4' sections and can be mounted on the wall vertically or horizontally. If you require a larger system, you can install as many sections as you need. With a grid system, the accessory hooks, shelves, and baskets simply lock into place (with no tools required) to create the exact system you desire in a matter of minutes; and the system setup can be changed as often as you want. A complete grid system can be designed from $100 upward, depending on the number of grids, hooks, shelves, and baskets you need. This system is available at Organized Living® stores and at www.organize-everything.com.

FIGURE 4.15
This grid system is easy to install and easy to adjust for your basic storage needs. (Photo courtesy of Schulte®.)

Multicomponent Storage Systems

A multicomponent storage system is one composed of a variety of types of storage units and options, including upper and lower cabinets, shelving, drawers, workbenches, pegboards, and other hanging solutions.

The O'Sullivan Coleman® Renegade™ four-piece garage system shown in Figure 4.16 is a good value at just less than $500. The system includes a two-door base cabinet, a three-drawer base cabinet, a tall utility cabinet, and an easy-mount pegboard hutch with moisture-resistant adjustable feet. The laminate cabinets include some adjustable shelves and a steel tread plate center support rail for extra durability, with a 10-year manufacturer's limited warranty. These systems are easily assembled and are available at Target stores nationwide as well as from numerous online retailers.

FIGURE 4.16
The Coleman®
Renegade™ system
includes several fea-
tures found in higher
priced systems.
(Photo courtesy of
O'Sullivan Furniture.)

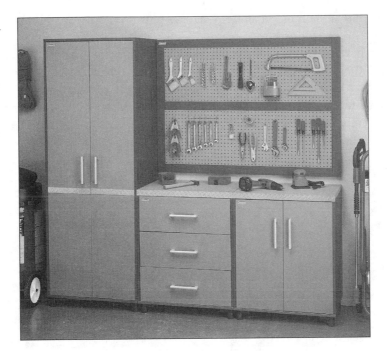

FIGURE 4.16
The Coleman®
Renegade™ system
includes several fea-
tures found in higher
priced systems.
(Photo courtesy of
O'Sullivan Furniture.)

Another O'Sullivan workbench and storage center, shown in Figure 4.17, is made of sturdy blue and blackstone laminate construction with a 1"-thick work surface. It includes a storage tower that can be attached on either side, a three-drawer base cabinet, and a two-door storage area with an adjustable shelf. With durable plastic feet and lots of pegboard to hang tools, this item's price of $200 makes it worthy of consideration.

FIGURE 4.17
This stylish blue stor-
age center and work-
bench is loaded with
features. (Photo cour-
tesy of O'Sullivan
Furniture.)

Truly one of the most outstanding values in this price category is the line of high-quality wood cabinets by Rubbermaid®, which includes a five-piece ensemble composed of a tall utility cabinet, a two-door wall-mounted upper cabinet, a two-door and a three-drawer base cabinet, as well as a workbench top, all for just under $500. Shown in Figure 4.18, the system not only features adjustable shelves and a metal kick plate, but also higher quality handles and adjustable feet for easy leveling. From color to design to application, Rubbermaid® has tied it all together in a system to be proud of at a price you can afford.

FIGURE 4.18
Rubbermaid® has gone the extra mile and paid attention to every detail to design an incredible system for an incredibly reasonable price. (Photo courtesy of Rubbermaid®.)

Creating a Storage System for Between $500 and $1,000

Although with careful planning and savvy shopping you can easily furnish a garage with the storage system you need for less than $500, it will be a challenging proposition for some and will ultimately depend on your individual circumstances. If you have a large garage and intend to outfit it with an entirely new system, more than likely you will need to spend more. If you are willing to cross the $500 threshold, you can create a more comprehensive and elaborate system using many of the manufacturers and components already mentioned, as well as some other higher priced systems.

tip If budget is a consideration, don't hesitate to mix and match from various systems to create the functionality you need. You might not need a complete modular system, and one or two components with some pegboard might be all you require. If you have already decided on a particular look and system that you like, another option is to buy the components you consider to be essential now and then add to the system later. You might be pleasantly surprised when you have put everything away and realize that these items are all you need!

Wall-Hanging System

Another incredibly versatile system that is easy to install is GarageGrids®, shown in Figure 4.19. Unlike other wall-mounted grid systems, the steel, epoxy-coated grids are currently available in 2'×6' sections, each covering 12 square feet. The soon-to-be-released 4'×6' sections can cover an entire wall very economically. The system comes with enough hooks, brackets, and baskets to get you started, and you can easily add more to create the storage solution you want. And the best news of all, you can change your system in seconds as your needs change. A starter system averages from $600–$700 and is available from the GarageGrids® dealer network, nationwide. To find a dealer in your area, go to www.garagegrids.com.

FIGURE 4.19

These large steel grids are durable, affordable, and can be rearranged in minutes. (Photo courtesy of GarageGrids®.)

Multicomponent System

You can mix and match the Coleman® Tuff Duty™ six-piece component system by O'Sullivan Furniture, shown in Figure 4.20, to create the ideal garage storage solution to fit your needs. The system features a moisture-, scratch-, and stain-resistant resin-based material with protective metal corners for added durability and adjustable shelves and feet. Backed by a 10-year manufacturer's warranty, it is easy to assemble and is an excellent value in this price range.

FIGURE 4.20
The Coleman® Tuff Duty™ system is stain resistant and is sturdy and durable, as its name implies. (Photo courtesy of O'Sullivan Furniture.)

Custom Garage Cabinet Systems

One of the latest trends to hit the garage storage scene are custom garage cabinets. Yes, you read that right. Companies are springing up in major metropolitan areas nationwide that offer very affordable, made-to-order wood, laminate, and melamine solutions built to your specifications at prices that you won't believe. This is an especially attractive option if you have a lot of windows and other barriers to plan around in your garage.

For less than $800 for a complete basic system, as shown in Figure 4.21, you can have scratch- and water-resistant cabinets installed along an entire wall (8' high and 10' long). Of course, the price goes up if you need additional cabinets or choose "extra" features, such as a custom finish, pull-out shelves, or hidden hinges. If this is a solution that seems ideal for you, look in your Yellow Pages under "Garage Storage Cabinets and Organizers" or online to see if there is a company in your area. Most companies offer free estimates and can install a system "in no time."

note If you can't find a company in your area that installs custom garage cabinets, do not despair. One Austin-based company, A Place for Everything (www.aplaceforeverything.net), will design your system over the phone and ship it directly to you. With easy-to-assemble instructions, it just doesn't get much easier than that.

caution All laminates and melamine surfaces are not created equally, so know what you are buying. Be sure when you are shopping to ask for a thermofused melamine that will not delaminate over time in humid climates.

FIGURE 4.21
This is one of the four basic finishes available in these sleek, custom-designed garage cabinets. (Photo courtesy of A Place for Everything.)

Complete Storage Systems for More Than $1,000

Although there are certainly many affordable options in garage storage solutions, the systems highlighted in this section are not for those on a tight budget. If you want to treat yourself and are determined to create the ultimate in garage décor, you will be delighted with several of the options in this category. New contenders are being added to the list more rapidly than ever before.

Wall-Hanging Systems

Both Elfa® and Schulte® sell systems you can install for less than $500 (see "Creating a Storage System for Less Than $500," earlier in this chapter), but their larger wall-hanging systems with all the accessories can easily top $1,000. The Schulte® freedomRail™ system, shown in Figure 4.22, includes shelving that comes in 30", 60", and 90" lengths, 12" and 16" depths, and adjustable components that come in 30" widths. Its GO-Boxes (Garage Organization Boxes) can be used as a cubby, a cabinet with doors, or a drawer unit. All kinds of hooks, racks and grids can be purchased to create exactly the system you want.

The Elfa® system, shown in Figure 4.23, includes white or platinum shelving, which can be purchased in 20" depths, in addition to 12" and 16", and the in-store staff at The Container Store® will cut the track, standards, and shelves to any length you need.

FIGURE 4.22
The Schulte® system pictured features grids, freedomRail™ shelving, and a variety of GO-Boxes to suit all your needs.

FIGURE 4.23
This Elfa® system has every accessory you need to store everything in your garage. (Photo courtesy of The Container Store®.)

The StoreWALL™ system, shown in Figure 4.24, is a slatwall alternative using easy-to-install PVC panels that come in five colors and accommodate more than 100 accessories made by companies such as Schulte®, The Accessories Group, and a host of others, to create the garage of your dreams. These waterproof and weatherproof grooved panels come in 4' and 8' lengths, can be cut and drilled just like wood, and provide a multitude of storage options for your garage. The more panels you use, the more of a finished look you will have. They won't crack or splinter. What's more, dents can be removed with a hair dryer, and cracks can be fixed with super glue!

There are several methods of installation, but using the color-matched screws is probably the easiest and creates the greatest load capacity. Several sizes of cabinets are designed to hang on the StoreWALL™-patented tongue-and-groove panel; the company also makes other cabinets that can be used with specially designed brackets. StoreWALL™ products are available through closet companies, garage storage dealers, and installers found on its website at www.storewall.com. You can also order the system by mail from Storic Storage Systems (www.storic.com).

FIGURE 4.24
This sleek slatwall system sports cabinetry as well as more than 100 accessories. (Photo courtesy of StoreWALL™.)

There isn't much that the makers of the GarageTek® haven't thought of in putting together the top-of-the-line versatile garage storage system shown in Figure 4.25. The lightweight, glossy thermoplastic Tekpanel® is weatherproof, waterproof, fireproof, and won't scratch, ding, or rust. It also carries a 10-year warranty. From the initial custom design by a local franchisee in your area to the professional installation, this company is a class act all the way.

The 10'-long-by-1'-high maintenance-free wall panels hold the widest variety of products seen in just about any garage system. Besides the usual hooks, baskets, shelves, and activity racks common to many systems, the GarageTek® system features heavy-duty shelves that can hold up to 200 pounds, an adjustable height workbench, see-through Tip-Out bins, and a Kid'z sports locker. Truly one of its more notable components is the Accessible Attic, shown in Figure 4.26, which is just over 4' wide, 4' deep, and 39" tall and can accommodate up to 1,000 pounds. Even the most ardent of packrats will have a tough time exceeding that weight limit! GarageTek's flooring solution comes in five colors and can be arranged in a multitude of patterns. It even includes a specially made cover to match the garage floor drain! To find a GarageTek® dealer in your area, visit its website at www.garagetek.com and prepare yourself for the ultimate in garage décor.

The professionally installed Tekpanel® system is lightweight, versatile, and offers a comprehensive storage solution that looks great. (Photo courtesy of GarageTek®.)

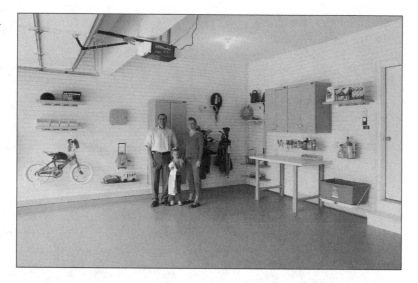

The Eurotec™ garage storage system by Comatec, Inc., shown in Figure 4.27, is patented worldwide and has been referred to as the ultimate in form and function. It's one of the more high-tech systems on the market (at a high-tech price). The system's sleek, contemporary wall units, storage shelves, bins, racks, cabinets, and hooks are made of durable heavy-duty aluminum and are easy to install and customize. Each shelf can support up to 200 pounds. For more information and to find a dealer near you, visit www.4garage.com.

FIGURE 4.26
The Accessible Attic shown here is the ultimate cabinet. It can hold up to 1,000 pounds. (Photo courtesy of GarageTek®.)

FIGURE 4.27
This slick and shiny aluminum European-styled system is easily customized and features unique accessories that attach easily and hold lots of weight. (Photo courtesy of Eurotec™.)

Multicomponent Systems

The Slide-Lok garage storage cabinet system, shown in Figure 4.28, is unique in that it offers eight basic finished cabinet components that you can mix, match, and stack to create a multitude of configurations. One of the major factors contributing to the great success of this system is that it is the only patented wood-based garage storage cabinet that carries a lifetime limited warranty. The durable, thermofused exterior comes in a choice of finishes to simulate real wood, and the adjustable shelves are made of medium-density fiberboard. The system has a custom-built look with concealed European hinges and fully adjustable legs for easy leveling. The patented dovetail assembly contributes to the strength of the cabinet and makes putting the system together an easy task. Not sure what design you want? You can find a dealer in your area to help you, or you can design your system online and order it directly from Slide-Lok at www.slide-lok.com. Either way, you can be sure you are getting a quality system that will provide a lifetime of service.

The Gladiator™ Garage Works system, by Whirlpool Corporation, is an innovative combination of high-tech modular units, cabinetry, and appliances, with powder-coated steel fronts that come with anywhere from a 10-year to a lifetime limited warranty. The workbench unit is 8' long with a solid, hard maple top, and it allows storage of up to three modular units underneath. Appliance options include a refrigerator, the Freezerator™, and a compactor, all with matching fronts. Gladiator™ has even developed a unique garage floor covering that rolls right onto your floor to give it a total finished look.

The system offers two types of wall-mounting systems, with easy-to-cut-and-hang GearTrack™ channels or GearWall™ panels. Both options mount over drywall or into wood studs, and the GearTrack™ channel mounts over masonry as well.

The GearTrack™ comes in 4' strips and accommodates all Gladiator™ wall accessories and gear boxes with a weight capacity of 75 pounds per linear foot. GearWall™ panels come in strips that are 1' high and 8' long and are installed one on top of the other. The rated weight capacity is 50 pounds per square foot. Although you can certainly design a basic garage system using some of the Gladiator™ products for less than $1,000, the system shown in Figure 4.29 will cost well over that amount. The systems are sold at Lowe's and Sears, or you can find a dealer in your area by visiting the Gladiator™ website (www.gladiatorgw.com).

Summary

I bet you did not realize there were so many choices in garage systems, did you? However, whether you use what you have or decide to purchase something new is not what is important. What matters most is that you have the storage systems you need to help you get organized—and even more importantly, to stay organized!

Even with the best storage system in place, the possibility exists that no matter how ruthless you are in getting rid of junk, your garage just might not be big enough to park your cars and store the things you need. In the next chapter, you will learn about alternative storage options, including the use of attics, basements, sheds, or offsite storage.

Analyzing Alternative
Storage Solutions

5

By now, you have laid out your new garage storage plan or decided that your current setup is working well. Perhaps you have purchased some new storage components to complement your existing system or you splurged and bought an entire new system. You are inspired and are already beginning to see the light at the end of the tunnel.

However, there is still one question that could well be lingering in the back of your mind. If you really do want to park two cars in your garage, where are you going to store the riding lawnmower and patio furniture during the winter, and the snow blower and snowmobile during the summer—not to mention the pool equipment and the table saw you use only a few times per year? If you are challenged for space, one thing is for sure: You cannot hang a riding lawnmower on the wall to get it out of the way, nor can you carry it down the stairs to the basement if you have one.

No matter how well organized you already are or intend to be, or how ruthless you are in getting rid of things you don't need, the fact remains that you just might not have the amount of space necessary in the garage to adequately store everything you need. In this chapter, you will discover the many alternative storage options available if your garage just isn't big enough for everything you need to keep. You will learn how to determine whether a shed is an appropriate option for you and, if so, how to select the right one to fit your needs. In addition, you'll learn some important considerations before choosing where to place it. The chapter also reviews the advantages and disadvantages of using attic and basement storage as well as provides some great storage tips for those who use them. If you are considering offsite storage, you will appreciate this chapter's guide to selecting the proper facility and determining how much space you will need. Finally, you learn about portable storage containers and how to determine whether this alternative is right for you.

To do list

- ☐ Decide whether you need a shed.
- ☐ Determine how you'll use the shed and choose one to suit your needs and budget.
- ☐ Choose windows, roofing, shutters, locks, and other accessories.
- ☐ Choose an appropriate site and install your new shed.

Choosing and Installing a Shed

Before you incur the additional expense of securing offsite storage or haul things up to the attic and forget that they are up there, a shed could very well be the most logical and realistic solution to achieving your goal of parking both your cars in the garage. Do not think of this as admitting defeat, as it might be your best option for those larger hard-to-store items such as the snow blower, your motorcycle, or the five bicycles your family enjoys taking to the lake in the summer. You might even already have a shed, but you hadn't thought of using it in this way because it is full of junk and stuff you just threw out there because you didn't know where else to put it!

Another reason a shed is a viable alternative for your pool equipment, riding lawn-mower, and other lawn and garden supplies is that your garage might have poor accessibility to the backyard. In Chapter 2, "Understanding the Organizing Process," you learned the importance of storing things near where they will be used, so they will be conveniently located and easy to access. It doesn't make good sense to store all the pool supplies in the garage if that location doesn't offer clear and convenient access to the pool, and you must walk all the way around the house to get the supplies. If you're an avid gardener and own a multitude of pots and potting supplies, a garden shed can be a great help in keeping your garage space clean and saving you a lot of extra steps.

Sheds and outdoor storage buildings are not solely used for storage anymore. They are a cost-effective solution that can be used for a variety of purposes, including workshops, studios, utility rooms, and children's playhouses, to name a few. As stated earlier, you must first decide how you intend to use the space, and that will make your choice of which shed to get much easier.

When you have determined that a shed is a good solution for your storage or workshop needs, you must consider a number of factors to select the best shed for your purposes. These include the type and size of shed you require as well as the features and accessories you want the shed to have. If you live in an area that experiences frequent tornados or hurricanes, consider spending more for a heavy-duty shed. Once again, much of this will depend on your intended use of the structure and your budget. The information in the following sections can help you make your choice.

Do You Need a Shed?

So, how do you determine whether you need a shed? The most important questions to ask yourself are, how do you plan to use the space and what specifically do you plan to store in the shed? If you don't have a lot of large items that are troublesome to store in your garage and you aren't really clear how you would use a shed, then be wary of getting one because it will simply become an "overflow garage" and eventually will look worse than your current garage does now! By answering the following questions, you will have a much better idea of whether a shed is the right choice for you:

- Would your current garage work better if you didn't have to accommodate the lawnmower, edger, wheelbarrow, weed eater, snow blower, and other large equipment?
- Is your garage becoming overrun with lawn and garden supplies, including tools, pots, bags of potting soil, and so on, that would be better stored in another place?
- Would having a shed make a lot of things you use in the yard more convenient to access and easier to put away?
- Is one of your hobbies beginning to overtake the garage so that there isn't room to store everything else?
- Would removing seasonal items such as patio furniture, pool equipment, sleds, snow blowers, and large outdoor decorations relieve a lot of your current garage congestion?

If you can honestly answer one or more of these questions with a resounding "yes," a shed could very well be the answer to your storage dilemma. Remember that only the more expensive sheds are insulated, so you will need to be careful what you store in one. Humidity and temperature extremes can cause mold, mildew, and rust, which can damage your patio furniture cushions and any other items that could be susceptible. A good rule of thumb is that if you wouldn't store a particular item in an attic, you probably shouldn't store it in a shed either. You will also want to purchase a good lock, especially if you are storing pool and other toxic lawn and garden chemicals out there.

caution Before you run out and purchase a shed, you must first determine whether you need a special building permit or if there are deed restrictions in your neighborhood or development that prohibit you from having one. Check the building code regulations and restrictive covenants in your city or area before you buy and build your shed.

Choosing a Shed Type

The three basic types of sheds are metal, vinyl, and wood. Your budget and aesthetics will be a major factor as to which one you decide to buy. All are available at home improvement stores nationwide and at shed dealers located in major metropolitan areas.

An aluminum and galvanized steel shed, as shown in Figure 5.1, is generally the least expensive, with prices starting as low as $400. While these choices might be more basic and simpler in design, they are utilitarian, durable, and available in a variety of styles, colors, and sizes to fit most budgets.

FIGURE 5.1

This metal shed represents one of the most cost-effective structures to gain additional storage space. (Photo courtesy of Arrow.)

Sheds with vinyl siding tend to be more maintenance free, and the panels are resistant to dents resulting from hail and other weather extremes. Also, these sheds include many color and roofing options.

Some of the more familiar barn-like structures are made of wood and can be painted to match the color of your house.

All these types of sheds come in various sizes to match your budget. Understanding how you plan to use your shed will be the key factor in deciding how large it should be. If you plan to use it as a workshop or hobby area, you will need it to be tall enough for you to stand up and move around in. Be sure to get a shed that is large enough for your current and future storage needs, because you will certainly find more uses for it once it is installed.

tip Depending on the type of shed you choose, you might be given a choice of roofing styles and colors. A gable or peak roof is most desirable because it provides the extra headroom you will require if you plan to actually work or store taller items in your shed. If you can, choose a roof style and color that most closely blends with your home.

If you are on a limited budget, several molded resin options by Rubbermaid® can be purchased for between $100 to $300, depending on size and amount of storage space you require. The Rubbermaid® Slide-Lid shed, shown in Figure 5.2, has almost 100 cubic feet of storage space, and the floor supports up to 1,300 pounds to accommodate a wide variety of items. The lid slides back to provide easy walk-in access, and it's lockable.

FIGURE 5.2

This molded resin shed is ideal for storing bicycles and all kinds of outdoor lawn equipment. (Photo courtesy of Rubbermaid®.)

If you have limited space in your yard, you might consider the unique Westminster five-sided shed by Spirit Elements, Inc. (www.spiritelements.com) shown in Figure 5.3. It will fit easily into any corner of your backyard or garden. The shed is made of kiln-dried, clear Scandinavian pine with a tongue-and-groove roof and floor included. With two windows and double doors, the shed is easy to construct and comes ready to paint or stain. It's priced at less than $2,000 and can be shipped anywhere.

FIGURE 5.3

This five-sided pine shed comes with its own floor and will fit well in the corner of your yard. (Photo courtesy of Spirit Elements.)

The Sierra by Spirit Elements, Inc., shown in Figure 5.4, is more than a shed—it's a multiuse structure that is sure to be the envy of your neighbors. Made of rough-sawn fir siding, this structure features two non-opening glass windows, cedar window boxes, shutters, and a door. The Sierra is priced at less than $6,000 and is available in many sizes and with a variety of customizable options. The kit is delivered in seven easy-to-assemble sections to make installation a breeze. The Sierra can be used as a backyard retreat, poolside cabana, or the ultimate children's playhouse.

Choosing Features and Accessories

Be careful to understand what is included in the price of your shed kit and what is considered to be an extra. Although a few sheds will come with a floor kit included, most will not, and this can add anywhere from $75 to $250 to the total cost. Most shed kits come with shingles, but some do not and you will have to purchase them as an extra. Some manufacturers include a window or two, whereas others make them available at an additional cost.

You will need to give careful consideration to the selection of the doors and windows to your shed. If you are going to be storing large items, you will want to consider an extra-wide opening with sliding or double doors. Some shed kits come with windows, shutters, and flower boxes; others do not. Windows are important not only to add to the aesthetics of your shed, but also to increase natural light sources and ventilation if you plan to work in there.

Other ways to customize and accessorize your shed include the installation of ramps to facilitate moving large equipment in and out of it, as well as cabinetry and shelving for more organized storage, or a workbench if you are planning to spend much time working inside. Some manufacturers offer lofts that you can install to maximize your storage capacity or additional vents to increase air flow and circulation.

Sheds come with a variety of locking options, and you will want to be sure you outfit yours with a good lock to protect the things you store and keep out uninvited visitors. You might want to consider having the lock keyed to match your house. Also, check with your insurance agent to be sure that coverage for the contents of your shed is included in your homeowner's policy.

Installing Your Shed

Selecting a convenient and accessible location for the placement of your shed is critical to ensuring you will get the maximum benefit from your purchase. Choose a spot on level ground with good drainage, preferably in a shady spot that will blend into the landscape. Avoid high-traffic areas. If you plan to store large equipment in the shed, make sure there is enough room to maneuver the equipment and move it in and out of the shed.

Do not let the fact that most shed kits require assembly deter you from getting one if this is a viable storage solution for you. Most dealers have installers who not only deliver the shed to your location, but also install the floor or foundation and assemble the shed.

To do list

- ☐ Learn the pros and cons of storing items in a basement or attic.
- ☐ Understand what types of items are appropriate for basement or attic storage.
- ☐ Learn guidelines for proper and safe attic/basement storage.

Utilizing Your Attic or Basement for Storage

I am confident you will agree that the garage can quickly become an out-of-control dumping ground of clutter if you don't actively stay on top of it and have a storage system that works. (That's probably the primary reason you bought this book, right?) Hopefully, you will heed my warning and believe me when I say that this danger applies doubly to the attic and to some extent the basement as well.

Many of you work hard to embody the concept that if you haven't worn or used something in the past year or two, you should get rid of it. Yeah, you struggle now and again and make exceptions for sentimental things and expensive items, but you are trying, and I commend you for it. But I also know that some of you have a different way of looking at things. Your approach is that if you haven't used it in a while, you can always stick it up in the attic or down in the basement, and it will be there when you need it... someday. If this solution sounds familiar, I strongly recommend that you reevaluate your strategy. Stashing unused items "just in case" is exactly why attics and basements tend to get out of control so quickly. Do you really think your daughter will want to wear your old wedding dress? And even if she does, what are the chances it will fit? With baby equipment manufacturers continually striving to make their products safer, most of what you are storing for your grandchildren is fast becoming obsolete and might not be safe anymore.

You know the old saying, "Out of sight, out of mind." A vast majority of my clients forget about their items once they are stored and out of view, and they don't discover these items again until they move. In some cases, they forget to take items stored up in the attic with them when they move and leave their "valuables" behind. So, why does this happen? If a person deems something important enough to be saved and stored, why would he or she just forget about it? The reason for this is simple:

As tempting as it is to use attic storage, it is often difficult to access and not very convenient. So what often happens is that people put stuff up there and simply forget about it.

Is Your Attic a Big, Black Hole?

Attic storage can be inconvenient and unsuitable for many types of items. If you are lucky enough to have a finished attic, with a real door and adequate headspace and a floor covering the upper-story ceiling joists and insulation, you won't face many of the most common difficulties of attic storage. This kind of setup is more common in new-home construction, as well as in many older (pre-1940s) homes. (Unless your attic is climate controlled, however, you will need to consider other issues of safe storage, as you learn later in this chapter.)

The majority of people with attics aren't so lucky and must access their attic one of two basic ways: through a ceiling door that pulls down with a fold-down ladder or through a simple ceiling opening (often located in a closet) that requires a portable step-ladder. I don't know about you, but this does not sound like a convenient storage area to me! If you have this kind of attic access, you dread going up there to retrieve anything and make every excuse why now is not a good time to do so. In the winter it's too cold, and in the summer it's too hot. When you finally do decide to venture up there, the sloping roof line prevents you from accessing much of the space without stooping or crawling. Compound that with the fear of hitting your head on exposed roofing nails, putting your foot through the ceiling below, breathing in all that insulation and getting it all over your skin, disconnecting the alarm, telephone, or cable wiring… not to mention my worst fear of all, running into a rodent. Well, it just isn't most people's idea of a good time.

Because the unfinished, difficult-to-access attic is the norm, I tend to refer to the attic as "the big, black hole" and typically recommend that homeowners store very little up there except perhaps leftover building materials from a remodel and things that are virtually impervious to being nibbled on, dripped on, and otherwise ruined or destroyed from extreme temperature fluctuation. Now, I recognize that, like it or not, some of you are short on space and have no other reasonable choice than to use your attic for additional storage of items. And the good news is that if things are stored properly and wisely, the attic can be a legitimate and practical storage alternative. Just promise me—and more importantly, yourself—that items that are broken or you no longer have a use for will be given away, donated, or tossed and won't make their way up there, okay?

Has Your Basement Become an Extension of the Mess in Your Garage?

Those of you who have a basement know that it can easily turn into a garage annex and a gigantic collection of many years of postponed decision making. Unfortunately, the more space you have, the more stuff you acquire. This is a fact of life. Although all that useable space is a blessing to some if used wisely, it can be a curse to many. Just like in the garage, you are wise to divide the basement into defined work and storage areas, such as laundry, utility, workshop, and storage. This will make it much simpler to get organized and stay organized.

Although a basement is certainly easier to access than an attic, unless it has a door with access to the outside, it will not solve the problem of where to store larger items such as a riding lawnmower, a snow blower, and a motorcycle because there is no way to get them down there. There is still a set of stairs to deal with in getting things in and out of the basement. In many cases, these stairs can be steep and narrow and will restrict the size and weight of things you can store in the basement, which often translates into whatever lands down there, stays down there. In addition, other issues to consider are dampness, flooding, and all kinds of insects, which can make storing things in the basement a real challenge.

However, if you are challenged for space in your garage and are determined to use it for the purpose it was intended, your basement can be the answer to your prayers for storing seasonal items and decorations, sporting goods, camping equipment, and many other things that are used only occasionally. The good news is that you will not need to buy another book to organize it. Most of the suggestions I have given you for organizing your garage in Part I, "Garage Organizing Basics," and the step-by-step instructions you will learn in Part II, "Creating Storage Centers: Everything Needs a Home," can be applied to the basement as well. Just take my advice and do not tackle both the basement and garage at the same time, okay? I want you to finish organizing your garage first, so you can be proud of your accomplishment rather than feel overwhelmed with more work ahead.

Things You'll Need

- ❏ Storage containers (plastic boxes or tubs, acid-free boxes, garment bags, rolling racks, and so on)
- ❏ Labeling system
- ❏ Dehumidifier (electronic or hanging)
- ❏ Cedar blocks or liners
- ❏ Plywood sheets and insulation (if necessary)

Smart Storage Tips for Attics and Basements

Storing items safely in your attic or basement requires special care and consideration because of the extreme storage conditions present. Water and moisture are your main enemies, followed by wide temperature fluctuations and bug and rodent infestations. The ideal storage temperature for most things is between 60 and 75 degrees Fahrenheit, whereas an optimal humidity range is between 50% and 60%.

When storing clothing, be sure it is laundered or dry cleaned beforehand, which will make it much less attractive to moths. If you don't have the luxury of constructing a cedar closet in your basement, clothing stored in vinyl garment bags on rolling garment racks works well, as do plastic storage boxes with small cedar blocks placed inside. If your basement is damp and proper care is not taken, your clothes will begin to smell musty over time.

caution It is risky to store things in cardboard boxes for several reasons. If a box gets wet and this goes undetected, the items inside will mold and mildew. Cardboard boxes are also an open invitation for an invasion of silverfish, roaches, and bookworms (no pun intended). One of their favorite meals is eating the glue in book bindings, and they will gnaw through the cardboard box as an appetizer to get to them. In addition, a silverfish will lay one to three eggs a day and can live up to three years. Do the math. Use plastic storage containers for maximum protection, but if you insist on using cardboard boxes, keep them off the floor!

Storing clothing in the attic should be avoided whenever possible. Excessive heat can break down certain clothing fibers, and temperature fluctuations can cause condensation, which causes clothing to mildew. If you have no other alternative than to store clothing in the attic, be sure to use air-tight containers to protect them. Consider using cedar blocks to create a hostile environment for insects that could be attracted to the natural fibers.

If you have an unfinished attic, the fastest and easiest way to increase your useable attic storage space is to lay a "floor" in it. Buy several 4'×8' sheets of plywood of 1/2" thickness and nail them to the ceiling joists, working your way out from the attic opening. Be sure to measure the size of your attic opening to determine whether you will need to have the plywood sheet cut in half or purchase another custom size from a home improvement store. It's a great idea to put some fiberglass insulation between the joists before nailing the plywood down; however, be sure that the insulation does not exceed the thickness of the joist, as it will become matted and defeat the purpose. If you plan to store extremely heavy items in the attic, it would be wise to consult an engineer to be sure your ceiling joists were made to support that kind of weight.

If dampness in your basement is a problem, purchase a dehumidifier with a drain tube directed to the outside to eliminate the need to empty the reservoir or risk it overflowing. Be sure to periodically inspect the tubing for any blockage. An inexpensive method for controlling dampness is placing activated charcoal in containers strategically located throughout the basement. If dampness continues to be a persistent problem, it could be well worth your time (and money) to determine the cause and remedy the problem now. By waiting, you could possibly be creating a more expensive fix later.

Here are some other tips for the safe storing of your belongings in your basement or attic (for more information on this topic, see "Weathering the Elements" in Chapter 1, "Where Do I Begin?"):

- The foundation of your home should be properly graded to ensure a dry basement.
- Use acid-free boxes for documents and photographs and plastic storage tubs for clothing and seasonal items.
- Don't pack books too tightly because they need some ventilation.
- Create an inventory of what you store so that even though things are out of sight, they won't be out of mind. Put one copy of your list in a clear plastic sleeve and attach it to the inside of the attic door. Be sure to label your storage containers well. For more information about labeling, see "Labeling the Contents" in Chapter 2.
- Check stored items regularly and detect problems in the early stages before things become ruined.

Keep stored items a minimum of 18" from furnaces, hot water heaters, and other electrical or gas appliances. Also, consider installing smoke, carbon-monoxide, and radon gas detectors.

To do list

- ☐ Decide whether you need offsite storage.
- ☐ Determine how much additional storage space you need.
- ☐ Choose an offsite storage facility or portable storage option that meets your needs.

Considering Offsite Storage

Here is what usually happens with offsite storage: Just as I warned about attic storage, when your things are stored "out of sight," they also tend to be "out of mind." And offsite storage is even less convenient than attic or basement storage, because you have to make a trip just to access your storage area. It is much easier to continue to pay the offsite storage bill each month than it is to drive there and make a final "keep or toss" decision about the stored goods.

Before you decide to rent an offsite storage unit, think long and hard about what you will be storing there. Ask yourself this very important question: Is the storage really worth the money I will pay each month—and what is more likely to turn into years—or will the amount I pay to store the items quickly surpass the value of the items themselves? You might very well come to the wise conclusion that offsite storage is just not economically practical or sensible.

I rarely advise people to pursue this option unless there is no other reasonable alternative and it is only for a limited amount of time. However, there are certain conditions under which I have recommended using offsite storage:

- You have inherited or been given furniture and other personal items from a family member and want to save them for your children.

- You plan to move to a larger home in the near future.

- You are faced with a temporary move and will be living in smaller quarters for a limited period of time and you can't take all your possessions with you.

tip — *Barry's Best*

Many people who put their home on the market need to "declutter" their house and garage to make them look roomier and more attractive. This process is often referred to as *home staging*, which has become a booming industry. Offsite storage is a great solution because you can pack up things you don't need and try living without them while you wait for your house to sell. If you find that you don't miss these items, get rid of them and don't even think about taking them to your new home.

POSTPONING THE INEVITABLE

Obviously, many people feel that they have legitimate reasons to use offsite storage, as it has become a multimillion-dollar industry, with more of these facilities being built every day. If your idea of organizing the garage is transporting most of it to an offsite storage facility, however, I advise you to carefully think this through. You are creating double work for yourself, taking on a needless expense, and postponing the inevitable. Although some people truly need to keep more things than their home storage space can accommodate, I have entered many storage units filled with worthless items that the owners eventually donated or threw away.

By prolonging the decision to dispose of these items, my clients spent hundreds of dollars per year in storage fees and put themselves through much mental anguish. Before you put anything in offsite storage, be sure that keeping these items will be worth the extra effort and expense and that you are not merely putting off an inevitable decision.

Selecting an Offsite Public Storage Facility

Once you have decided that there is no other option than to utilize an offsite public storage facility, you need to consider several things to ensure you make the right choice.

Renting the Right Amount of Space

The first rule is not to get more space than you need. The storage spaces you can rent come in all shapes and sizes, so how do you know which size you need? Several considerations will influence your space requirements. If you plan to load the space and retrieve things only occasionally, you can pack your items tightly and economize with a smaller space. However, if you plan to be in and out of your space often and will be constantly moving things back and forth between your home and storage, you will want to leave yourself ample room to maneuver and will need a larger storage space.

Using Table 5.1, you can roughly estimate how much space you require.

Table 5.1   What Size Storage Unit Do I Need?

Dimensions	Square Footage	Will Hold the Equivalent Of:
5'×5'	25 square feet	Boxes, small pieces of furniture
5'×10'	50 square feet	Studio apartment, one small bedroom
5'×15'	75 square feet	One large bedroom
10'×10'	100 square feet	One to two bedrooms
10'×15'	150 square feet	Two to three bedrooms

Storage units are available that will hold twice as much as those listed here, but let's be optimistic and hope that you don't have that much currently being stored in your garage and that you are willing to get rid of some of it.

Prices will vary greatly depending on geographic location, the size of the space required, and the amenities you are looking for. Many of the larger national public storage facilities offer online rate quotations and lucrative move-in specials.

Choosing a Good Facility

Not all public storage facilities are created equally, and here are the basic things you should be looking for before choosing one that is right for you:

- How safe and secure is the facility? Is there an onsite manager and is it well lit? You will want to know if the site has 24-hour surveillance. This will be very important if you plan on accessing your unit at night.
- Does the facility have a sprinkler system and smoke alarms?
- Is the facility clean and free of any signs of rodents?
- Do you need a climate-controlled unit? Keep in mind that in most public storage facilities, you will pay extra for a climate-controlled space. If you are storing items that could become damaged from temperature extremes, moisture, and mold, you have little choice but to incur the extra cost. The last thing you want to do is incur the costs for offsite storage only to discover later that your possessions have become ruined.
- Does the facility have standard hours of operation or does it provide 24-hour access with a security gate for which you will be given a special access code? The frequency with which you need access to your unit, as well as your work schedule, will determine whether this is an important consideration for you.
- Where will your unit be located? Understand that prices vary depending on whether your unit is downstairs or upstairs and has drive-up or hallway access. The frequency with which you expect to access your unit, the price, and the convenience desired will determine how important this is to you.
- What are the terms and length of the rental contract? Hopefully, this is a short-term storage solution, so the last thing you want to do is lock yourself into a contract period that is longer than you need.
- Can you purchase additional insurance for your possessions? Find out if insurance is included as part of your rental agreement or if you have the option of purchasing it.

> **tip**
> If you own a home, you would be wise to check with your insurance agent to determine whether your homeowner's insurance covers the possessions you are storing offsite.

Utilizing Portable Storage Containers

A relatively new alternative to public mini-storage facilities is capturing the public's attention and has gained increased popularity within the past five years. Many companies now will deliver portable storage containers to your home or place of business, as shown in Figure 5.5. You load the containers yourself at your convenience. Then you have the option of storing the containers on your property or having them picked up and stored at the company's warehouse—or even moved to another city! Depending on the volume of items you are moving, this can represent a great cost savings. However, be aware that the cost for moving insurance can be more expensive for this mode of transportation because you packed the pod yourself rather than having a professional do it.

FIGURE 5.5

Portable self-storage containers, like this one from At Your Door, are delivered to your home or business. (Photo courtesy of At Your Door.)

Three of the larger companies offering this service are PODS (Portable On Demand Storage; www.pods.com), Door to Door Storage (www.doortodoor.com), and At Your Door Self Stor! (www.atyourdoor.com). These companies have been very successful with this concept and are rapidly expanding their operations into metropolitan areas nationwide. Packing a pod is easy, as illustrated in Figures 5.6 and 5.7.

FIGURE 5.6

Packing a pod is a simple process. (Photo courtesy of Door to Door.)

This storage pod is partially packed. (Photo courtesy of PODS.)

Be aware that not all portable container storage companies are created equal. One of the most important questions to ask is what kind of lift they use to pick up the pod and load it on the truck. Some companies use hydraulic lifts, whereas others use forklifts. This can make a big difference in how much your belongings get shifted around. Depending on what you are storing, you might prefer a hydraulic lift to minimize shifting of your contents.

Remember that these companies do not have staff that will help you pack and load the container—that's your job. If you select this storage option and you are not physically able or choose not to load your own container, you should seriously consider hiring a professional organizer to help you. Some of them specialize in garage organization and will be able to assist you with this project. To find a professional organizer in your area, go to the NAPO (National Association of Professional Organizers) website at www.napo.net and click "Find an Organizer" to access the automated referral system.

As with any storage solution, portable storage has both advantages and disadvantages, as shown in Table 5.2.

Table 5.2   Advantages and Disadvantages of Portable Storage

Advantages	Disadvantages
Convenient pickup and delivery.	You have fewer sizes of containers to choose from than with traditional offsite storage facilities.
You can take your time loading.	You incur a delivery and pickup fee.
If you're storing the container on your property, it's more convenient than an offsite facility.	Some companies require you to call and schedule access to warehouse-stored containers in advance.
You pack and unload only once.	It could be more costly than traditional offsite storage, depending on your needs.
You avoid renting a truck and driving somewhere.	You must hire someone to load the storage container if you're not able, as opposed to a traditional moving company.
You can ship a loaded container to another city.	Insurance can be more costly because you (rather than a professional mover) pack the items.

Summary

At this point, you should have a pretty good idea if there is enough room in your garage for all your storage needs. If there isn't, you've determined whether you need to get a shed or secure offsite storage, or make more efficient use of your attic and/or basement. In this chapter, you learned some of the possibilities and limitations of utilizing any of these alternative storage areas and how to store items safely and properly in those locations. You've also learned how to assess the use of an offsite storage facility, whether you choose a traditional facility or one of the new portable storage container options.

As you finish this chapter and the first part of this book, you now have all the information you need to organize each storage center of the garage. You have learned the basic organizing principles, methods of storage, and the wide array of storage systems available. Whether you have already purchased a new storage system or have decided to wait and reward yourself when you are finished with the sorting and purging portion of your garage organizing project, you are now ready to move on to Part II.

Each chapter of Part II will help you apply what you have already learned to organize a particular storage center of the garage. Read each chapter as you work through the process, or just choose the chapters that are relevant and apply to you. After you work through one or two of your storage centers, you will become an old pro and wonder why you waited so long to get organized. So, turn the page and let's keep going!

Part II

Creating Storage Centers: Everything Needs a Home

In this chapter, you will learn how to determine what kind of workbench you need, if any, and where to put it. You will discover the many options available to you, ranging from items you may already have that can be used for this purpose to workbenches you can purchase to complement the rest of your garage system. Finally, the chapter offers an easy step-by-step guide for organizing your workbench after it's in place.

To do list

- ☐ Determine the size of workbench you need.
- ☐ Choose the best location for your workbench.

Assessing Your Workbench Requirements

The first thing you need to evaluate is how often you have used your existing workbench in the past year or two, or how often you would use a workbench if you had one. If you find that you work on only a couple projects per year, you probably don't need a full-time standing workbench because it will more than likely become a clutter magnet, and a less permanent solution could work equally well. Although this might not be an ideal solution, it will free up more storage space, which can be utilized year round. However, if you have the necessary space, I highly recommend having a workbench if for no other reason than to have a place to glue or nail something back together, work on a craft project, or polish your shoes.

note If you don't need a "full-time" workbench and plan to use a folding table, collapsible workbench, or a sturdy piece of wood or a door placed across two sawhorses, be sure to put it away after each project. Otherwise, you will find that it becomes a permanent piece of your garage landscape. Make sure that you include a convenient place to store your makeshift workbench in the garage plan you created in Chapter 1, "Where Do I Begin?" This way, it is easy to access and yet out of the way when you're not using it.

Determining the Best Size for Your Workbench

Analyze how handy you are and how often you find yourself engaged in "do-it-yourself" projects around the house. If you spend every weekend on a new project (and you finish them all!) and really enjoy it, then allowing more space for a workbench and tool storage area makes great sense. A workbench that is 6' long or more

Making Your Workbench Work

Perhaps you're thinking you don't need to read this chapter. You are not handy, you have yet to complete one project you have started, you don't build or fix things, and you are quite happy to keep it that way. That could be true, but at one time or another, everyone has something that needs to be repaired, fixed, assembled, glued, or mended, and we need an appropriate place to do it. And where is the most logical place to do these tasks? That's right...at the workbench in the garage. Just as you would not think of designing a kitchen without a sink or furnishing a bedroom without a bed, you should not overlook the workbench—an essential component for most garages.

Although the type and size of workbench as well as the amount of money you might spend on one will be greatly influenced by your "handyman quotient," you still need a place to perform messy tasks and quick repairs, and I doubt you want to designate your dining room or kitchen table for this purpose. A workbench doesn't need to be elaborate or expensive, as long as it's functional and fits within the available space. Besides, having a workbench is more efficient—not to mention safer—for performing a number of home repair tasks (I can't imagine anyone attaching a vise to the edge of the kitchen counter to saw a piece of wood in half).

is ideal. However, if the thought of puttering and fixing something yourself sounds about as much fun as cleaning leaves out of your gutter or sorting a jar of screws, you can get by with 5' or less.

The height and depth of a workbench is just as important as its length. Although the standard height of workbenches is anywhere from 30–36" tall, a workbench that is 40–42" high often works better for several reasons. When a workbench is taller, it reduces the need to bend and lessens the stress on your lower back. It also allows for more out-of-the way storage underneath. However, if your workbench is going to serve the needs of several members of your family, you might want to compromise by choosing a height that works for everyone who'll use the bench.

The depth of a workbench should be at least 20" (more is preferable), especially if you plan to permanently attach a vice and other tools to it. A 3" overhang on the bench top is ideal if you plan to attach clamps and vises; otherwise, 2 1/2" is fine.

Choosing the Ideal Location for Your Workbench

You must take into account several factors when deciding the optimal location for your workbench. If your garage is narrow and barely wide enough to accommodate two cars, you have little choice but to locate your workbench on the back wall. Otherwise, you are likely to dent your car door or have little room to exit the car. Also, if the car is parked in the garage, you will have little or no room left to work at the workbench. However, if your garage is not very long or your cars are exceptionally long, you might have the same problem locating the workbench on the back wall as well. Though not ideal, you may have little choice but to back your car out when you want to use your workbench.

One important factor is good lighting. My personal preference is to place the workbench under or near a window or another natural source of light. If your garage does not have a window or if this location is not suitable, you should locate your workbench closer to the garage door so you can open it for additional lighting, as well as for increased ventilation. Even if you have a good natural light source, you will still need another light source, preferably located at the workbench itself for up-close work.

Another important consideration is convenient access to an electrical source of power. Even if you don't have any power tools that require electricity, you will need electricity for the direct lighting necessary for close-up work or when working at night, or you might need to plug in a soldering iron or a glue gun for a craft project. If you have no alternative than to use an extension cord, be sure it is a heavy-duty one and is properly grounded to avoid electrical shock (see the sidebar titled "A Plug for Safe Power Sources.")

Another important factor to consider is placing your workbench where you will have the easiest physical access to it. Most people have little choice but to place their workbench against the back wall to conserve space and still be able to pull their cars into the garage. An optimal solution, if you have enough space, is to place your workbench perpendicular to the wall, as illustrated in Figure 6.1. This arrangement affords you the opportunity to move freely around the workbench and approach it from all angles, yet it still allows you to mount cabinets and pegboard on the wall for tool storage (discussed further in Chapter 7, "Tackling Your Tools") and have drawers underneath.

FIGURE 6.1

Placing your workbench perpendicular to the wall allows for easy access and lots of room to work.

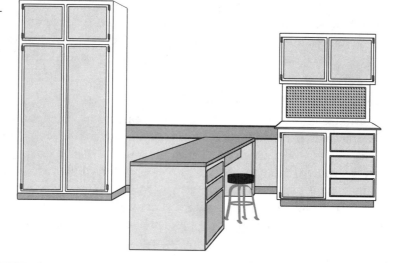

A PLUG FOR SAFE POWER SOURCES

Be sure you locate the workbench near electrical power receptacles—this will be especially important if you use corded power tools. If you find an ideal place for a workbench that is not located near an outlet, hire a licensed electrician to determine whether a GFI (ground fault interrupter) outlet can be installed near the bench. A GFI outlet has a built-in "trip" to interrupt the power supply and prevent you from receiving an electrical shock resulting from a loose wire or contact with water when working with a power tool plugged in to the outlet.

This installation might require the electrician to run exposed conduit, but it will be well worth the expense and far safer than running a heavy-duty extension cord along the floor to get electrical power to where you need it.

To do list

- ☐ Find out how to make a workbench from desks, chests, or other materials you own.
- ☐ Learn about the different types of manufactured workbenches and how to choose one that matches your preferences, needs, and budget.

Selecting a Workbench That Works

There are several important considerations in selecting a workbench that works, including how you are going to use it as well as the stability and storage options it provides. Some of these are matters of convenience, whereas others directly affect safety.

If you are going to use a vise and saw lumber, you will need a workbench that is very stable and can support this kind of task. You wouldn't be able to use a vise on many portable or makeshift workbenches, nor would you even want to try. Think about the danger and drastic consequences that could occur if you were using a power tool and your workbench moved even the slightest bit.

If you work on projects that require a lot of space, then selecting a workbench with a large work surface is critical. And while having a large enough work surface is very important, you will be very disappointed if you have plenty of workspace with no place close by to store the tools you use when you are working there. Organization is all about convenience, and you want to have the tools you use at the workbench to be right there where you need them. This will help to ensure that they will be put back where they belong when you are done using them. As you can well imagine, a wide variety of workbench styles are available—from the homemade to the high tech. You might already have the makings of a workbench that will suit your needs nicely. If you need to buy a workbench, you have plenty to choose from. With prices ranging anywhere from less than $100 for a small, easy-to-assemble, particle board configuration with pegboard sides and a single shelf underneath, to elaborate benches costing $1,000 or more, the choice you make will largely depend on your budget, what you like, and what you need.

Creating a Workbench from Items You Already Own

As mentioned in previous chapters, finding new uses for items that have just been taking up space is a great way to help organize your garage. If you need a workbench but don't have the money to buy one, there are several items you might already have that can be redeployed for this use. An old office desk or chest of drawers can make a great workbench, if you don't need a lot of workspace and don't plan on spending much time at it. Even a small section of old kitchen cabinets, as shown in Figure 6.2, will work with a piece of laminate countertop cut to fit as the work surface.

Having plenty of drawers beneath the workbench helps free up lots of workspace. Figure 6.3 shows one of my favorite homemade workbenches, which comes fully equipped with drawers of all sizes to keep needed items handy. The workspace is expandable, too. I can simply open a drawer and put a board on it, and I will have more surface area on which to spread out my work.

You can recycle many items as accessories for your workbench, as well. For example, you can use a plastic hanging shoe bag near your workbench to hold tape measures, small hand tools, screwdrivers, various kinds of tape (electrical, plumber, masking), and often-used small items. Use your imagination to create a useful and economical workbench and tool storage area.

FIGURE 6.3
This homemade beauty utilizes drawers of different sizes to keep tools and other supplies close at hand.

Portable Workbenches

Portability can be an essential feature if you don't have an ideal place for a workbench and want to give yourself total flexibility as to where you work. Portable workbenches answer this need, but make sure they can stand up to the task you require. Many of them are not as sturdy as a permanent workbench, so read the manufacturer specifications and warnings carefully. You might not be able to attach a vise, use power tools, or support as much weight on them as you would like. However, one significant advantage is that you can fold them up when you are finished and store them vertically on or against the wall until the next time you need them.

The Coleman portable workbench, shown in Figure 6.4, can be purchased for around $100. This inexpensive solution can provide the workspace you need, where you need it—in the house, the garage, or even outside.

FIGURE 6.4
This portable workbench with locking wheels gives you the option of working anywhere you roll it. (Photo courtesy of O'Sullivan Furniture.)

The Sauder rolling island shown in Figure 6.5, is part of the Hot Rod® collection and is priced around $350. It includes two heavy-duty drawers with additional storage space underneath.

FIGURE 6.5
This hot red and silver pearl portable island has a Truck-Tough® poly-coat work surface. (Photo courtesy of Sauder®.)

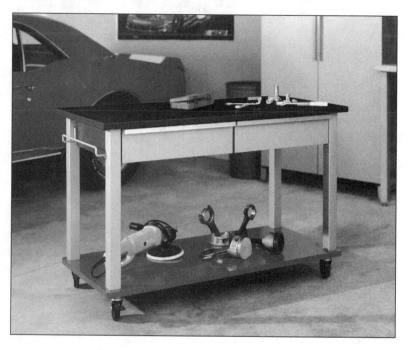

Some of the portable workbench styles even come with a variable-height top and a built-in vise. No matter what other options or features you choose in a portable workbench, make sure the wheels can be locked so that the workbench remains steady while you are working.

tip
If you have a permanent workbench but are in occasional need of a portable one, you can erect a makeshift workbench in a matter of minutes by placing a sturdy piece of wood on two sawhorses.

Wall-Hanging Workbench Systems

A wall-hanging workbench is a great option for those who have limited space. This type of workbench hangs right on the wall, offering a greater amount of unencumbered storage space underneath because it doesn't have legs to get in the way. Before you purchase one, be sure that you read and understand all the manufacturer recommendations, including weight restrictions.

The workbench in the integrated Schulte® system shown in Figure 6.6 attaches to the wall with brackets just below the Schulte slotwall. In addition to the workbench, this system features a little bit of everything, including the Activity Organizer shelf solution kit and wall-mounted laminate cabinets. Schulte® products are available at Organized Living stores nationwide. To find a dealer in your area, visit www.schultestorage.com.

FIGURE 6.6
This wall-mounted workbench featured below the slotwall completes this multi-faceted system and provides a variety of storage solutions. (Photo courtesy of Schulte®.)

The wall-hanging workbench options shown in Figures 6.7 and 6.8 hang on StoreWALL™ slatwall PVC panels and are available in 4', 6', and 8' lengths and 2' depth. They range in price from $350 to $650, including the brackets. The two-drawer units are priced separately beginning at $150. To learn more about the StoreWALL™ system, see Chapter 4, "Selecting Storage Systems." The Dura Top work-bench units are available through Storic Storage Systems (www.storic.com) and Garage Interiors of Michigan (www.gimich.com).

Modular Workbench Systems

A modular workbench system is one that includes many types of storage methods and features in one package. Purchasing a system of this type makes shopping easy and gives you a variety of storage options at a very affordable price. Not only does the system feature a workbench work surface, but it can include any combination of pegboard, drawers, cabinets, and shelves. Such systems often include built-in light-ing and electrical power outlets.

FIGURE 6.7

The 4' version of this handsome workbench sports two drawers and the Dura Top working surface. (Photo courtesy of StoreWALL™.)

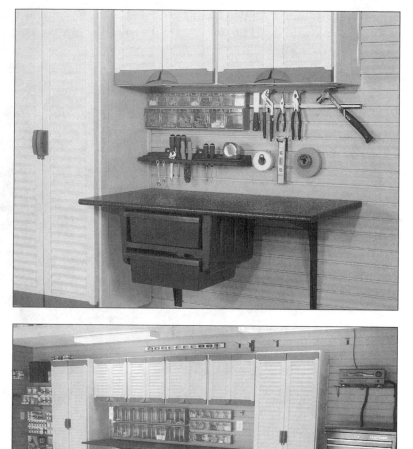

FIGURE 6.8

This complete StoreWALL™ system, featuring the 8' Dura Top workbench, places everything within easy reach.

If you are looking for versatility, Crown Wall by Acclaim Design & Profiles, Inc. (www.homeorganizers.ca) offers an interlocking vinyl panel system, shown in Figure 6.9, that provides versatility and style, all rolled into one. The "slotted" grooves of the lightweight panels will accommodate bins, plastic and melamine shelves, and a multitude of accessories, including heavy-duty epoxy-coated metal and plastic hooks and storage racks. Sturdy molded resin cabinets can be incorporated into the system on the wall or on the floor.

A custom-made workbench, such as the scratch- and water-resistant workbench shown in Figure 6.10, can be designed to fit your exact desired dimensions and requirements. Whether you need drawers, cabinets, or open shelving, look in the Yellow Pages for your city under "Garage Storage Cabinets and Organizers" or online and you should be able to find a company that can build exactly what you want for a price that you may find surprisingly affordable. If you can't find a company in your area, do not despair. One Austin-based company, A Place for Everything (www.aplaceforeverything.net), can design your workbench over the phone and ship it directly to you with easy-to-assemble instructions.

The Sauder beauty shown in Figure 6.11, from the Hot Rod® collection, costs just under $600 and features a heat-, stain-, and scratch-resistant Truck-Tough® poly coat work surface and a routed surface edge to contain spills and hold tools in place. The system features a pegboard hanging wall, a fluorescent work light, a power strip with three outlets, and a phone jack. The 5' long upper cabinet has two adjustable shelves and attaches to the top of the workbench. To find a Sauder dealer in your area, visit www.hotrodbysauder.com.

FIGURE 6.11
This heavy-duty workbench and lock-able upper cabinet assemble easily and feature adjustable levelers. (Photo courtesy of Sauder®.)

The new MasterSuite Garage System by ClosetMaid®, shown in Figures 6.12 and 6.13, offers a finished, custom look that will make you smile every time you drive your car into your garage. The laminate components of this system are designed to resist staining, warping, and chipping and come in a variety of sizes that can be mixed and matched to fit your exact storage requirements. All the utility, wall, and base cabinets are available in 24" and 32" widths, and the base cabinets come with adjustable legs and four drawers or a drawer and enclosed shelf space. In addition, the cabinets can be stacked to create floor-to-ceiling storage space. Dealers for the MasterSuite series can be found on the ClosetMaid® website at www.closetmaid.com.

FIGURE 6.12

This basic package includes a workbench with a utility cabinet and a four-drawer base cabinet. (Photo courtesy of ClosetMaid®.)

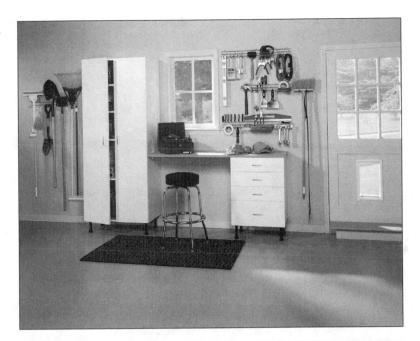

FIGURE 6.13

This deluxe system includes stackable cabinets and a work-bench surface that is 1" thick and can stand up to a lot of abuse. (Photo courtesy of ClosetMaid®.)

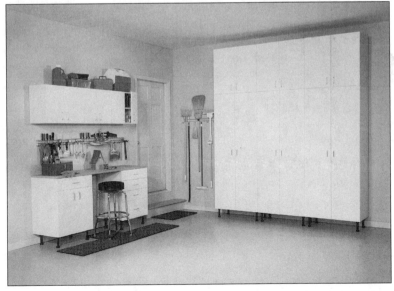

To do list

- ☐ Dispose of unnecessary items in and around your workbench.
- ☐ Sort the stuff you intend to keep at your workbench into groups of like objects.
- ☐ Reduce collections of like items by keeping only those you need and will use.
- ☐ Choose locations for storing your items.
- ☐ Place items in their new homes, using storage boxes or other containers, pegboard, drawers, and labels, as appropriate.

Organizing Your Workbench

Whether you have decided to purchase a new workbench or are happy with the one you already have, let's talk about how you are going to organize it. In this section, I provide a quick recap of the process you'll use to get your workbench area organized and ready to provide you the efficient, useful work area you need.

note In Chapter 2, "Understanding the Organizing Process," I outline the organizing process in detail. I highly suggest that you read that chapter if you haven't already. It thoroughly explains all the steps you need to follow to be successful with any organizing project and includes lots of examples.

Things You'll Need

- ☐ Boxes labeled "Keep," "Donate," and "Garage Sale" (if appropriate)
- ☐ Trash can
- ☐ Storage containers
- ☐ Labels and a permanent marker or label maker (if desired)

Step 1: Reducing the Volume

If you are like most homeowners, your workbench surface is covered with everything from tools to cans of paint, items waiting to be fixed, supplies you have bought and never used, and countless other things that you aren't even quite sure how they got there. The first thing you need to do is remove everything from the area that obviously does not belong there...one by one. Have your trash can ready and if the item needs to be trashed, throw it away and don't think twice about it. If it belongs in another storage center of the garage (lawn and garden or sporting goods), move the item there now. If it is something that you want to donate or sell, put it in the appropriate box or make piles in the center of the garage floor or in the driveway. Don't create the piles too close to the workbench because you will need the space nearby as you work through step 2. If you can't make a quick and easy decision, save the item for step 2.

Step 2: Removing What Remains

Now that you have eliminated everything that obviously doesn't belong on your workbench, remove everything else and clear the space. Lay these items on the floor space near the workbench. I realize you will be putting many of these items right back, but this is a necessary part of the process for you to understand how much space you have available to work with and how much of what you remove is realistic to keep. It will also give you an opportunity to clean the top of your workbench. As you remove these items, some of you will begin to sort the items into groups on the floor, putting like things together, and others will choose to do this as the next step in the process.

Step 3: Sorting

Sorting is fundamental to the organizing process because it enables you to see how much of a particular item you currently own and also facilitates the purging and weeding process. As you sort, you will begin to group like things together. Some people prefer to sort as a two-step process and find it helpful to initially sort items into boxes labeled "Keep," "Donate," and "Garage Sale," and then sort the items in the "Keep" box later. Others will prefer to lay all the items they will keep out on the floor nearby and sort as they go. It really doesn't matter which way you do this, as long as you can easily see what you have. Of course, you will need to have a trash can nearby for the things that nobody would want under any circumstances.

Once you have sorted everything, it will quickly become apparent if you have eight hammers and 14 pairs of wire cutters, and you can make an informed decision as to how many of each item you wish to keep and what you want or need to get rid of depending on how much space you really have. This is also going to help you when you put the items back, because you will want to keep like things together, which will make it so much easier to find them when you need them. For additional help on sorting tools, see Chapter 7.

Step 4: Purging and Weeding

An integral part of the sorting process is purging and weeding or more simply put, getting rid of the excess things you no longer need. Some of you may choose to do this simultaneously as you sort; others will prefer to sort first and toss things later, and still others might do a little bit of both. Once again, this is just a matter of personal preference and what comes naturally to you. It doesn't matter how you do it, as long as it gets done.

TRIMMING YOUR TOOL COLLECTION

So, how do you decide what to keep and what to get rid of, either by tossing, donating, or selling? In Chapter 2, you will find a thorough list of questions to answer to guide you through this process, but here's a quick recap:

* When was the last time you used this item?

* Is the item in good working condition and safe to keep?

* Is the item still useful and relevant?

* Do you have a logical place and enough space to keep the item?

* What is the worst thing that will happen if you get rid of the item?

More specifics related to the purging and weeding of tools will be discussed in Chapter 7, where you'll also find help in understanding which tools you really need. Once you have completed the purging process, Chapter 13, "Getting Rid of Stuff," provides you with a lot of recycling options and suggestions of places where you might consider donating these items.

Step 5: Selecting and Replacing Items in Their New Home

Having completed the sorting and eliminating process, you are now ready to place the remaining items in their new home. In the workbench area, your choices are many and will only be limited by the system you currently have or have chosen to buy and the quantity of what you are actually storing. Some of the items will go back in the exact place they were, while you will undoubtedly choose new homes for others. Ideally, your workbench area will be equipped with cabinets above and below, as well as some drawers and possibly a pegboard or slatwall for the tools you use most often.

Step 6: Containerizing and Labeling

As you place items to be stored in drawers or in cabinets, you will want to appropriately containerize them and label the containers. The goal of organizing any area is to make the end result a lasting one. As you've learned in previous chapters, by creating and using storage containers, the items you've sorted will remain sorted, so you do not have to repeat this process any time soon. Your tools and workbench accessories will be easy to find, your workbench area will remain uncluttered and useful, and the tasks you perform on the workbench will be more efficient and less frustrating. Obviously, you won't containerize things you hang on a pegboard. Also, the larger the item, the less likely you will need to containerize it.

note For more information on the available methods of storage and selecting the most appropriate home for what you are storing, refer to the tables in Chapter 3, "Reviewing Storage Options." For more information on the types of storage systems available, you will want to peruse Chapter 4, "Selecting Storage Systems."

But how do you know what kind of container to use for which item? This basically depends on what you will be storing in the container. There are so many choices, but one basic rule of thumb is that the container must be large enough to hold similar items together in one place and allow a little room for growth; but not be so big that it takes up a lot of unnecessary room. And, of course, the container needs to fit the space where you plan to put it! The most important thing to remember is that you can't make a serious mistake when containerizing your possessions, so start with what you think is best and know that you can always change your mind down the road.

tip If your budget is tight, you'll find lots of suggestions in Chapter 2 for containers you might already have hanging around that will adequately get the job done.

Remember, labeling containers is very important and will help you more easily find things when you are looking for them. If you have a lot of drawer space in your workbench, you might not need as many containers as if you were using open shelving, but depending on what is being stored in the drawers, you might choose to use drawer dividers instead. Be sure to label the tops or fronts of the drawers themselves for easy identification of their contents.

Summary

In this chapter, you have learned how to select a workbench that will work for you and the various points you need to consider in determining the best location for it. Even if you decided to keep the workbench you already have, you have learned how to maximize its usefulness and the important steps necessary to get it organized.

Now that you have organized your workbench, it's time to tackle your tools. If you have a limited number of them and own only the basic essentials, you might have already included this as part of the steps to organize your workbench. However, if you are an ardent craftsman or have every tool known to mankind—whether you know how to use it or not—the next chapter will illustrate for you the various tool storage options and assist you in determining which ones you need to organize your tools.

Tackling Your Tools

7

Whether you are an avid woodworker, an ardent do-it-yourselfer, a hard-core handyman, or you don't know the difference between a Phillips or slotted head screwdriver, everyone needs some tools for the occasional home repair. Even if you who have vowed never to fix anything yourself and insist on calling a service professional for even the smallest job, you still need some tools for minor operations such as hanging a picture, changing a light switch plate, or removing a vent cover or a door from its hinges.

Analyze how handy you are and how often you find yourself working on do-it-yourself projects around the house. If you spend every weekend on a new project (and finish each one!) and really enjoy yourself, then providing plenty of space for a workbench and tool-storage area makes great sense. However, if the thought of puttering and fixing something yourself sounds about as much fun as cleaning leaves out of your gutter or sorting a jar of screws, you might not need as many tools as you currently own.

In Chapter 6, "Making Your Workbench Work," you learned how to choose and install a workbench that's right for you. By now, either you have decided to keep the one you have or you have already bought a new one. This chapter focuses on the storage of hand tools and power tools in and around your workbench as well as in other important locations (we talk specifically about lawn and garden tools in Chapter 10, "Weeding Out Lawn and Garden Clutter"). After a very brief guide to deciding which hand and power tools are

In this chapter:

* Getting a grip on which tools and how many tools you need
* Sorting and ridding yourself of the tools you don't need
* Identifying options of where to donate unwanted tools
* Storing your hand and power tools
* Determining the storage system that will work best for you

important for you to have, this chapter goes on to explain how to organize the tools you already own and covers the many options you have for storing them.

Back to Basics: Tools That People Need

If your workshop has become a graveyard for unfinished projects and your tools have a layer of dust on them an inch thick, you might want to reconsider just which tools you really need before you begin to organize what you have.

Here's a list of basic tools every homeowner (or even apartment dweller) should own for the occasional do-it-yourself project:

Hammer	Glue gun
Small level	Staple gun
Wire cutter	Measuring tape
Adjustable wrench	Cordless drill (battery operated)
Pliers (regular and needle nose)	Vise-Grip locking pliers
Heavy-duty scissors	Utility knife
All-purpose saw	Putty knife (plastic or metal)
Hacksaw	Swiss Army knife
Screw drivers (assortment of Phillips and slotted head)	

You might require other hand tools as well, of course, depending on the types of special projects you commonly tackle. However, the tools in the preceding list are "must-haves" for just about everyone.

The right power tools will save you much time and elbow grease. A cordless rechargeable screwdriver with interchangeable bits (Phillips and slotted head) is a must unless you invest in a cordless drill, which will serve double duty. If you decide to purchase a cordless rechargeable drill, get one with a minimum of 16 volts of power. It costs only a few dollars more but you will appreciate having the variable speeds and extra power when you need it—trust me on that!

To do list

- ☐ Collect all your tools together and decide which you will keep.
- ☐ Clear out the area where you'll store your tools.
- ☐ Sort the tools into groups.
- ☐ Decide what to do with the tools you don't need.
- ☐ Organize the tools within the storage area.

Organizing Your Tools

If you haven't already read Chapter 2, "Understanding the Organizing Process," I would encourage you to do so. That chapter outlines the organizing process and thoroughly explains all the steps you need to follow to be successful with your project; it also includes lots of examples. The following sections offer a closer look at these organizational steps, as they specifically apply to the task of organizing the tools in your garage.

Things You'll Need

- ☐ Box or basket to gather tools up
- ☐ A flat sorting surface such as the floor, a workbench, or a table
- ☐ Trash can and labeled boxes for sorting
- ☐ Tool-storage system(s)

Step 1: Gather Up the Tools and Reduce the Volume

If you are like most people, you don't have just one hammer, you probably have five. If screwdrivers were gold bars, you would be rich. The only problem is that they are scattered throughout the kitchen drawers, the utility room, the garage, the trunk of your car, and the basement. Not only do you not know how many screwdrivers you have, but you can never find the right one when you need it.

The first thing you need to do to organize your tools is to gather them all up and see what you have. This will mean making a quick trip through the house and everywhere else you have tools stashed and collecting all of them, including those in your toolbox, in one central location (such as the top of your workbench or on the floor nearby). You are going to be amazed at how many screwdrivers and hammers you have accumulated over the years.

Once you have all your tools in one place, it is time to make the quick-and-easy decisions. If a tool is broken, worn out, badly rusted, hasn't been used in years, and you can't identify an immediate need for it, get rid of it. Why would you want tools to repair screens if you only do it once every five years, if that much? Doesn't it make a lot more sense not to own and store the equipment and supplies yourself, but to take the screens somewhere to be repaired when they need it? Besides, if you are like most people, the job will probably get done a lot faster that way!

Step 2: Clear the Tool-Storage Area

Now that you have made the easy decisions, it is time to remove all your tools from your workbench drawers, toolboxes, pegboards, hooks, and anywhere else they might be hiding and lay them out on a flat surface. Depending on the quantity of tools you own, you might be able to spread them out for sorting on top of the workbench or a table. And for those of you who have lots of tools, the garage floor will work great if you can find it; if not, use the driveway. The important things are to clear out a designated storage space so you can replace the tools in a more organized way and to give yourself plenty of room to sort.

Step 3: Sort Your Tools

Sorting is fundamental to the organizing process because it enables you to see how many of a particular item you currently own and it also facilitates the purging and weeding process. This is especially important when it comes to tools because you likely don't use them regularly and it is hard to remember what you have. You will be surprised when you lay everything out and see how many duplicates you have.

As you sort, you will group like things together and create areas for hammers, screwdrivers, wrenches, files, and so forth. This not only speeds up the purging and weeding process, but it also helps you when you put the tools back to know how much storage space you need for each kind of tool. By storing like things together, you make it so much easier to find the tools you want when you need them.

If you have a very limited quantity of tools, you might find it helpful to sort them directly into boxes labeled "Keep," "Donate," and "Garage Sale." If you have more, you will prefer to lay everything out and sort on the floor or driveway. It really doesn't matter which way you do it, as long as you can easily see what you have. Of course, have a trash can nearby to toss the tools you and nobody else would want under any circumstances.

Step 4: Eliminate the Tools You Don't Need

An integral part of the sorting process is purging and weeding—or, more simply put, getting rid of the excess tools you no longer need. You may choose to do this simultaneously as you sort, you may prefer to sort first and toss things later, or you may do a little bit of both. Once again, this is simply a matter of personal preference and whatever comes naturally to you. It doesn't matter how you do it as long as it gets done.

 **note** If a tool works, wait until you lose it or it breaks before you buy a replacement. You don't need to have a mini hardware store in your garage.

So, how do you decide which tools to keep and which ones to get rid of (either by tossing, donating, or selling)? In Chapter 2, you will find a complete list of questions to ask yourself that will guide you through this part of the process, but here's a quick recap as you examine each tool:

- When was the last time you used it?
- Is it in good working condition and safe to keep?
- Is it still useful and relevant?
- Do you have a logical place and enough space to keep it?
- What is the worst thing that will happen if you get rid of it?

Once you have sorted everything, it will quickly become apparent that you have, say, eight hammers and 14 pairs of wire cutters. Then, you can make an informed decision as to how many of each item you wish to keep and what you want or need to get rid of, depending on how much space you actually have.

Resist the temptation to keep too many duplicates. The average person doesn't use his or her tools enough to wear them out, so unless you are planning to lose them, it just doesn't make sense to have too many extras, unless you want to stock a portable toolbox for the house or car.

 You might choose to have a set of workbench tools as well as a portable toolbox or a tool drawer in the house for convenience when working on smaller projects. This way, you don't have to go out in the garage every time you need a tool for a quick fix. If you decide to do this, color-code the handles of the tools that will go in your toolbox or the drawer of your house with a marking pen to make it easier to put them back where they belong.

If you have more than several of the same tool, keep the newest, the one that's in the best condition, or the one you like the best, and get rid of the rest. You might need two of something, perhaps even three or four if you have decided to have several sets of tools in different locations, but you definitely don't need 14!

note Once you have completed the purging process, Chapter 13, "Getting Rid of Stuff," provides you with a lot of recycling options and suggestions of places where you might consider donating your items.

FINDING GOOD HOMES FOR YOUR TOOLS

If you find yourself running across tools you don't need, but they are just too good to throw away, consider these options:

* Give them to a neighbor.
* Make a set of tools for your children who are going off to college or moving into their first apartment or house.
* Donate them to a high school or local theater group, a vocational group, or Habitat for Humanity.
* Sell them on eBay. Hand-made and vintage tools are in high demand and go for prices that would astonish you.

Step 5: Place Your Tools in Their New Home

Once you have completed the sorting and elimination process, you are now ready to put your tools back in a well-organized arrangement. That way, when you need a #2 Phillips screwdriver or an adjustable socket wrench, you will know exactly where to look. In Chapter 3, "Reviewing Storage Options," various storage methods are discussed, along with tips on selecting the best home for a particular item.

Hanging Your Tools

One of the most logical ways to store tools is to hang them, and one of the most popular means is the use of pegboard. If you need instructions on how to install pegboard, see Chapter 3. If you don't have that many tools and need only a small amount of hanging space, you can buy a framed piece of pegboard at most home improvement stores and mount it above your workbench.

One of the most significant advancements in the world of pegboard is the Bunjipeg™. This unique innovation holds tools of any size or shape firmly to the pegboard with no metal hangers, hooks, or adapters needed, as shown in Figure 7.1. You just slip your tools behind the elastic cord, which is held in place with forked pegs spaced at the intervals you select. The Bunjipeg™ system is easy to move and rearrange as your needs change and is currently only available online with sets priced from $9 to $20. For more information, see Chapter 3 or visit www.bunjipeg.com.

FIGURE 7.1
Bunjipegs™ hold all
your tools firmly in
place, eliminating the
need for metal hang-
ers and hooks. (Photo
courtesy of
Bunjipeg™.)

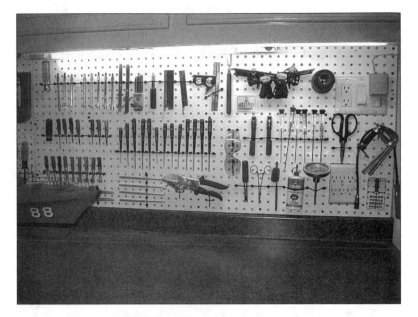

FIGURE 7.1
Bunjipegs™ hold all
your tools firmly in
place, eliminating the
need for metal hang-
ers and hooks. (Photo
courtesy of
Bunjipeg™.)

In addition to the use of pegboard are many other simple ways to hang your tools
that are not only economical but very inventive. I wish that I could take credit for
thinking of them myself; however, I must admit that many of them were not my
idea at all, but creative methods I encountered as I did research for this book. The
best part is that most of the items needed for this kind of tool storage can be found
buried in boxes of things you just couldn't bear to part with because you might need
them someday. Well, someday has arrived. If you don't have these items, I have no
doubt you will be able to find them in someone else's garage sale.

Figure 7.2 shows a clever way to hang clamps from a simple wooden towel bar
attached to the wall. Although this towel bar is made of wood, a retired metal or
durable plastic one could work just as well.

FIGURE 7.2
Would you have ever
thought to use an old
towel bar to store
your clamps? (Photo
courtesy of FayleSafe
Solutions.)

Another variation on the towel bar theme is to hang hammers and other hangable items from it, as shown in Figure 7.3. Pictured just above the hammers is a home-made holder for screwdrivers. You can make one yourself by drilling holes of various sizes at 2"–3" intervals in a piece of wood. You can use this type of holder for storing other hand tools as well.

FIGURE 7.3

This homemade wooden combo rack holds hammers, screwdrivers, and lots of other tools too. (Photo courtesy of FayleSafe Solutions.)

If you're not that handy and are challenged for space, all kinds of wall mountable tool holders can be purchased for less than $10. The multilevel tool rack shown in Figure 7.4 is made of polypropylene and won't bend, warp, or sag.

FIGURE 7.4

This tool rack holds up to 96 tools in just 2 feet of space. (Photo courtesy of Organize-Everything.com.)

Finding the exact type and size of saw you need is a breeze if you have them all mounted on pegs along the wall, as shown in Figure 7.5. You can achieve a similar result by mounting an inexpensive coat rack with hooks or by hammering sturdy nails into the wall at 2"–3" intervals. Whichever method you choose, be sure the pegs or nails are long enough to securely hold the handles of the saws so that they can't fall and injure someone. Also, mount them high enough so young children can't reach them.

FIGURE 7.5

Storing saws on the wall can be safer than laying them in a drawer. (Photo courtesy of FayleSafe Solutions.)

Many tools are made of metal and can easily be hung from a magnetic toolbar similar to the ones you commonly see in kitchens to hang knives. The 18" magnetic toolbar shown in Figure 7.6 can be mounted to studs and can hold anything from screwdrivers to lawn and garden tools.

FIGURE 7.6

The double magnetic strips on this toolbar securely hold all kinds of tools and gadgets. (Photo courtesy of Organize-Everything.com.)

Storing Tools in Drawers

Although hanging tools is a preferred storage option for maximum visibility and accessibility, it is not always feasible for a number of reasons, and alternative methods need to be considered. Although tools can certainly be placed on shelves, preferably in an enclosed toolbox or well-labeled container, another great option for storing them is in drawers. When tools are extremely heavy or an odd shape, as is the case for the large wrenches shown in Figure 7.7, drawer storage is the perfect choice. It is usually safer, too, because there is little danger of them falling. Tools with sharp edges, such as the saw blades shown in Figure 7.8, are good candidates for a drawer as well, although they can also be hung carefully on a hook or nail on a wall.

FIGURE 7.7
These heavy items store well in a drawer.

FIGURE 7.8
By storing saw blades in a drawer, you make it easier to keep them together and find the one you want when you need it.

With other tools, such as the wrench set pictured in Figure 7.9 and the wood and metal files shown in Figure 7.10, there just isn't a convenient or practical way to hang them up. By storing them in a drawer, it is much easier to keep the set together so that it will remain a set.

FIGURE 7.9
This freestanding rolling toolbox has lots of drawers and makes sorting different types of tools a breeze.

FIGURE 7.10
This old card catalog makes the perfect home for metal and wood files and hinges. (Photo courtesy of FayleSafe Solutions.)

Storing Power Tools

You have many options for the storage of power tools—you can hang them up, put them on a shelf inside a cabinet, place them out in the open or underneath your workbench, or put them in a drawer. Of course, your ultimate choice will depend on how many power tools you have and the storage systems available to you.

Because many power tools come in their own case, storing them on a shelf in a locked cabinet is my preferred choice for safety reasons. Remember, these are *power* tools, and they can be very dangerous if you have young children, who might decide to plug them in and "try them out." If you don't have a cabinet, store them on an upper shelf near the workbench and out of reach of little hands. The slatwall system shown in Figure 7.11 is a great example of how power tools can be stored safely on shelves and hooks.

FIGURE 7.11
This slatwall system utilizes a variety of hooks and shelves to keep power tools handy. (Photo courtesy of StoreWALL™.)

Whenever possible, store your power tools in the case they came with. This not only keeps the attachments and spare parts with the tool for your convenience, but it also helps to prevent them from getting lost. If a power tool did not come with a case or you no longer have it, use an old gym or bowling bag to store it and keep the pieces together. You can also cut a piece of old foam or use an old pillow for extra protective cushioning. Laptop computer bags also work well for this purpose, or even a labeled plastic storage container.

When possible, store the manual with the power tool and staple the purchase receipt inside. Some of these tools have extended warranties; if the tool malfunctions or breaks, you won't have to go searching for the receipt. Other options for manual storage include a magazine holder on a shelf or in a drawer. If you have a lot of manuals, consider storing them in the drawer of an old filing cabinet with alphabetized hanging files.

USING SOFTWARE TO ORGANIZE PAPER AND BOXES IN THE GARAGE?

If you own a lot of power tools, you might even want to use The Paper Tiger® filing system for storing the tool manuals.

The Paper Tiger® is a revolutionary software product that uses the computer to solve your problems with filing and managing paper and knowing what's stored in your boxes once and for all! Imagine being able to put your fingers on any tool manual, product warranty, sales receipt, project "how-to" instruction guide, or any one of the voluminous collection of plant-growing instructions and gardening articles you have saved over the years, in five seconds or less—guaranteed! You can use it to inventory each individual item inside all your boxed and containerized storage. No more guessing whether the item you're looking for is in the garage, attic, or basement. If you are an avid woodworker, you can even sort all your sandpaper in hanging file folders by type and grit! You'll spend less time searching and more time doing and being productive.

The Paper Tiger® is like having an Internet search engine for your filing system. The software is simple to learn, easy to use, and you will wonder

Photo Courtesy of The Paper Tiger®.

how you ever lived without it. It includes a "live" step-by-step tutorial and all the tools you need to solve your paper-storage problems in the garage—and everywhere else for that matter. For more information and to find an authorized consultant in your area, visit www.ThePaperTiger.com.

Photo Courtesy of Smead.

Another product worthy of consideration is the software product ARRANGE™ File Organization System, manufactured by Smead (www.Smead.com). A keyword search not only will help you find filed paper, but also electronic or scanned files and web pages too. You can even print your own customized, color-coded Smead Viewables® labels and tabs. ARRANGE™ can be purchased from an assortment of online retailers including Amazon.com.

☐ Decide the best way to store your tools.

☐ Choose the storage system that is right for you.

Choosing a Tool-Storage System

Many kinds of tool-storage systems are available on the market, and your choice will depend on your needs, your budget, and the amount of space you have. If you have not already read Chapter 4, "Selecting Storage Systems," which showcases the many types of garage storage systems available, or Chapter 6, "Making Your Workbench Work," which illustrates several options for tool storage in the workbench area, I would advise you to do so before making your selection. Rather than repeat all that information here, I have chosen to illustrate just a few of the many possibilities you might want to consider.

The slatwall system shown in Figure 7.12 integrates an assortment of tool-storage options already discussed in this chapter, including a variety of hooks, a multilevel tool holder, a magnetic tool holder, and adjustable shelves. Did you notice the snazzy custom holder for the wrenches? Bin storage is discussed more in Chapter 8, "Managing Nuts and Bolts: Pieces and Parts."

FIGURE 7.12
The adjustable storage options are endless with the StoreWALL™ system. (Photo courtesy of StoreWALL™.)

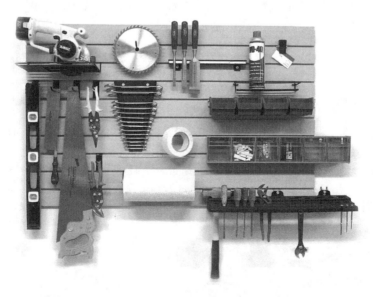

Figure 7.13 features a totally adjustable, aluminum tool-storage system available through Stacks and Stacks (www.stacksandstacks.com). It mounts to the wall and comes with shelves, hooks, holders, and bins to organize your tools with ease. It comes in two sizes, is available online, and is priced from $220–$300.

FIGURE 7.13

This unique wall-mount tool-storage system comes complete with all the accessories and enables you to organize your tools "in no time." (Photo courtesy of Stacks and Stacks.)

The Eurotec™ worldwide-patented garage system by Comatec, Inc., shown in Figure 7.14, takes tool storage to new heights. This floor-supported system, made of durable heavy-duty aluminum, evenly distributes the weight so that each shelf can support up to 200 lbs. This state-of-the-art system comes in six finishes, available in five colors, and is guaranteed not to rust. For more information and to find a dealer near you, visit the Eurotec™ website at www.4garage.com.

FIGURE 7.14
The wide assortment of hooks, shelves, and bins in this high-performance collection will hold any tool imaginable, giving you maximum flexibility and a lifetime of service. (Photo courtesy of Eurotec™.)

Summary

Now that your tools are organized, the workbench area is almost completely finished, but not quite. There is one more thing we need to devote our attention to before we can move on to organizing the other storage centers of the garage. Actually, it's more than one thing—it's a lot of little things. Chapter 8 will walk you through how to deal with your endless collection of nuts and bolts and pieces and parts. It is all good news, so don't despair. The end is in sight, and you are doing great!

Managing Nuts and Bolts: Pieces and Parts

I will be the first to admit that one of the most laborious and tedious tasks in organizing the garage is sorting nails, screws, nuts, bolts, and all those little pieces and parts that have accumulated over the years. Like many of you, when I assemble something and have some screws and other extra parts left over, I toss them into a jar or can, along with similar parts from other projects. The only drawback to this system is that it's not very efficient. Whenever I need a specific item or particular size of something, it involves dumping the entire contents of the jar or can out onto a flat surface and sifting through everything, hoping to find just what I need. The more "bits" I have, the more difficult this process is.

In this chapter, you will first decide whether it is important for you to sort your collection of nails and screws. If your answer is yes, you will learn how to successfully sort by setting guidelines and parameters and deciding to what extent you are willing to go to get these items organized. Once you've sorted these small connectors, you will be guided toward selecting the storage solution that best suits your needs.

To Sort or Not to Sort—That Is the Question

Wouldn't it be nice to have everything neatly sorted so that when you are looking for a 2" wood screw with a flat head, you would know exactly where to get one? Of course it would! But the real question is whether it's worth taking the time to sort through the years of accumulation to make this happen.

Depending on how large your "stash" is and how detailed your sort will be (for example are you going to sort not only by item, but also by length, type, and thickness?), sorting all those little pieces and parts you have been saving for years could take hours...even days! I don't know about you, but I just don't have the time or patience to make that happen.

Only you can determine how valuable your time is and how important it is to you to have these things perfectly sorted and organized. Here are some questions that will help you decide if it is even worth serious consideration:

- How often do you find yourself needing small items like these? If it's only once or twice a year, perhaps having everything all mixed together in one place works just fine.

- What kind of volume do you have? If the grand total is 30 or 40 pieces in a coffee can or jar and that's all you ever plan on having around, sorting really might not be necessary.

- If the little pieces in your assortment are easily distinguishable from one another, does it matter if they are mixed together in one place?

- If your nails, screws, nuts, and bolts are already separated from one another, is it really worth the additional time to sort them by type or size?

- Is this a good use of your time? Would it make more sense just to toss or recycle what you currently have (for example, by giving your collection to Habitat for Humanity) or sell it by the can at a garage sale and then start over by organizing everything you buy from now on?

If you decide that it is important to sort what you have, you might want to consider paying one of your children or one of your neighbor's children to do it. Even at a fairly young age, children can discern between a nail and a screw or a nut and a bolt. Not only will they appreciate the money, but it will teach them a valuable skill and help preserve your sanity. Just be sure that they are old enough and beyond the age of sticking little things in their mouth!

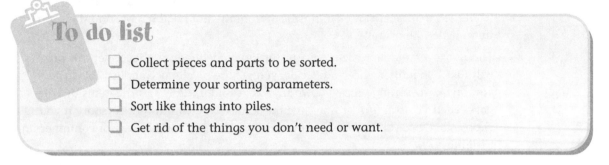

To do list

- ☐ Collect pieces and parts to be sorted.
- ☐ Determine your sorting parameters.
- ☐ Sort like things into piles.
- ☐ Get rid of the things you don't need or want.

Organizing the Pieces and Parts

If you are determined to organize your prized collection of pieces and parts and are not willing to part with them, here is a quick rundown of how to tackle this task if you want to just dive in and get started.

Things You'll Need

- ☐ Pieces and parts to sort
- ☐ A flat sorting surface (workbench, table, or floor)
- ☐ Plastic containers or cans to separate the sorted pieces
- ☐ Comfortable chair (optional)

Gather Up the Items

Many people store their nails, screws, nuts, and bolts in jars, cans, or some sort of container, so it should be easy to gather them up and place them all out on the workbench to begin the sorting process. If you already use a specially designed drawer unit to store these things, place that there as well.

tip When you're preparing to sort through your collection of connectors, make sure you have a comfortable chair and some music, because you could be sorting for quite a while.

Define the Parameters and Sort

The purpose of a sort is to group like things together to determine how much of a particular item you have and what is a reasonable amount to keep. This is what enables you to put things back in an organized way and locate them easier in the future. The question is, how detailed and extensive do you want the sort to be? Of course, you want to separate the nuts and bolts from the screws and the nails from the cup hooks, but how far do you want to go? Do you want to separate the wood from the metal screws, the Phillips head from the flat head screws, and then sort them by length as well?

The narrower and more defined your sorting guidelines are, the longer this process will take. No matter what you decide, you will be able to accomplish this faster if you break the sorting process down into steps and initially sort the items by category. Then you can further fine-tune the sort by type within that category if you choose to. Once you have set your guidelines, dump a can, drawer, or container and begin to sort.

Eliminate What You Don't Need

When sorting pieces and parts, it is difficult to assess the actual quantity you have of a particular item until you have completed the entire process. Of course, while you are sorting, be sure to toss any pieces that are obviously broken or rusty, and purge all those useless items you cannot identify, foresee any imaginable use for, or have held onto for years because you were sure you could use them for something and it would be a sin to throw them away.

Once the sorting process is finished, you should look at the quantity that remains and decide if you want to reduce it even further. The one thing working in your favor here is that these things are small and don't take up a lot of space, so if you can anticipate a future need, go ahead and keep them.

To do list

- ☐ Choose a storage system that suits your needs.
- ☐ Place your sorted pieces and parts into your storage system.

Storing Your Sorted Pieces and Parts

Now that you have completed the sorting process, you need to designate a home for the freshly sorted pieces and parts so they will stay organized. Even if you decided to get rid of all the screws, nails, and miscellaneous parts you have been saving for years, you will need a place to store the new ones that will creep back into your life.

You have a multitude of options for storing nuts and bolts, and your choice will ultimately depend on the quantity you need to store as well as your budget. The good news is that even some of the slickest options aren't very expensive at all and can be purchased at prices ranging between $15 and $40.

Things You'll Need

- ☐ Sealable plastic bags and clear plastic containers
- ☐ Clean, empty jars
- ☐ Coffee cans, cookie tins, cigar boxes, and other castoff containers
- ☐ Purchased storage containers

Economical Storage Solutions

You can use all kinds of common household items that cost you next to nothing to store screws and nails or nuts and bolts. Most of these storage methods are best suited to be placed in a drawer or sit on a shelf:

- Ziploc® bags
- Clear plastic containers with lids
- Clean, empty jars (olives, relish, condiments, spaghetti sauce)

USING BABY FOOD JARS FOR STORAGE OF NUTS AND BOLTS

My father was the first person I ever knew who had used baby food jars to store nuts and bolts, screws, nails, anchors, and tacks, and for many years, I believed he was the person who had invented this idea! Of course, I later learned that people began using this method shortly after Gerber bottled its first baby food for junior. And why not? It works so well, it was something almost everybody had, and it didn't cost anything extra.

Whoever thought of mounting the jars under a shelf was surely one of the first professional organizers, but he or she just didn't know it. It saves shelf space, you can't lose the lids, and because you can see through the jars, you don't have to label them.

Want to make your own? Simply nail or screw the lids of the jars under a shelf a few inches apart, and your storage system is ready to use, as shown in Figure 8.1.

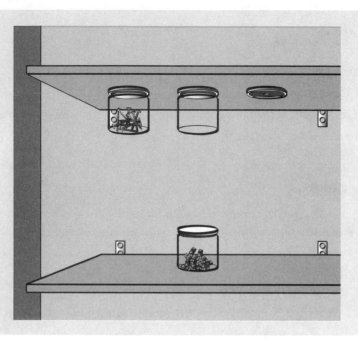

Items you can see through are best for storing nuts, bolts, washers, and screws. However, if you are determined not to spend any money, here are some things you can use that you probably already have:

- Coffee cans
- Cookie tins
- Cigar boxes
- Old kitchen canister sets
- Margarine, cream cheese, and cottage cheese containers

Because you can't see through the items in this list, be sure to label them clearly or tape a sample of the item(s) enclosed in the container on the outside. This is far more preferable to searching through each and every container when you're looking for something specific.

Homemade Storage Systems

The drill bits displayed in Figure 8.2 are just another example of homegrown ingenuity. Holes in a range of sizes have been drilled into the wood approximately 1" apart to accommodate the various diameters of the drill bits. After the wood shelf was attached to the wall, a piece of metal was added to hold the specialty bits.

FIGURE 8.2

It is easy to find the drill bit you need with this unique wall-mount system. (Photo courtesy of FayleSafe Solutions.)

Take a look at Figure 8.3; this has to be one of the more resourceful ideas I have seen for storing pieces and parts, and it works just as well as any store-bought solution. The neatly labeled drawers of this old printer's stand have been put to good use once again and hold a vast amount of nuts, bolts, screws, and washers.

FIGURE 8.3

This antique printer's stand is an imaginative, functional solution and an excellent example of taking something old and turning it into something new. (Photo courtesy of FayleSafe Solutions.)

Specially Designed Storage Systems

As mentioned earlier in this chapter, if you are willing to spend just a little money, you can purchase products created specifically for the storage of small pieces and parts. My favorite solution is the rugged, mini drawer storage units made by Akro-Mils shown in Figure 8.4, which contain anywhere from 16 to 64 polypropylene, see-through drawers. The unbreakable drawers can be subdivided and the unit can sit on a shelf, be stacked on top of another unit, or be mounted on the wall. The units are priced between $16 and $33 and are available at major home improvement stores and online at www.organize-everything.com.

FIGURE 8.4

These mini storage units with transparent drawers let you see what is inside and are available in all sizes to store all kinds of little items. (Photo courtesy of Akro-Mils.)

Another popular solution for the storage of small pieces and parts is the stackable heavy-duty AkroBins® made by Akro-Mils, shown in Figure 8.5. Available at major home improvement stores and online at www.organize-everything.com, these sturdy bins are guaranteed not to break or rust and come in a variety of colors. They are sold in sets ranging in price from $6 to $11.

If you have many sizes of the same kind of item, just being able to see inside might not be enough. Clear labeling of the individual drawers or compartments of each storage unit, as shown in Figure 8.6, will be critical in helping you put your hands on exactly the right part when you need it. For more information about labeling and label makers, see Chapter 2, "Understanding the Organizing Process."

These space-saving
stackable bins come
in a variety of sizes
and can sit on a shelf
or hang from special
racks. (Photo courtesy
of Akro-Mils.)

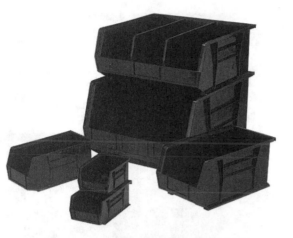

Labeling the large
drawers in this stor-
age unit makes it
easy to find the exact
size nail you need.

The Crown Wall shown in Figure 8.7, by Acclaim Design and Profiles, Inc., has several options for the storage of pieces and parts. Items can sit on a shelf or can be
directly inserted into the slotted grooves of the lightweight vinyl panels. For more
information, visit www.homeorganizers.ca.

FIGURE 8.7
This Crown Wall features several popular systems for storing nails, nuts, bolts, and other small items. (Photo courtesy of Acclaim Design & Profiles.)

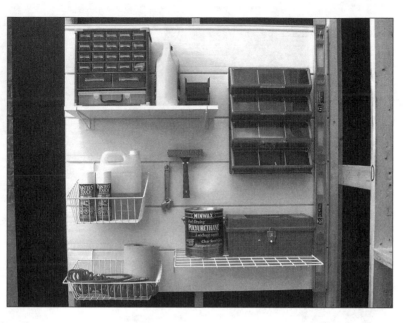

Portable Storage Systems

If you have a limited amount of small pieces and parts, you might be interested in the Carousel system by Emplast®, shown in Figure 8.8. It sits on a shelf but can be moved to the top of your workbench when you are working on a project. It features three rotating trays, which make it easy to find that special part you are looking for because you can see everything all at once. At slightly more than a foot in height and diameter, the Carousel is available online at www.organize-everything.com for $15.

If portability is an important feature to you, here are two great options for storing little pieces and parts that you can carry anywhere. The clear compartmentalized box shown in Figure 8.9 is just one of many sizes available. It enables you to see what is stored inside, eliminating the need for labels. The lids on these boxes fit tightly to make them spill proof, and many of them feature adjustable dividers to customize the compartment sizes to fit your needs. The boxes range in price from $5–$11 and are available at discount and home improvement stores everywhere as well as online at www.organize-everything.com.

tip *Barry's Best*

Have you ever picked up a little part and stared at it wondering, "What the heck does this belong to or where did this come from?" Of course you haven't! My advice is not to be too hasty to throw it away. Instead, allow one drawer or container for what I would label "Miscellaneous" or simply "?". You will know exactly where to go and look for that part when you discover six months later what it is or where it belongs. Periodically, feel free to discard something if it has been in there for a couple years.

FIGURE 8.8

This revolving carousel can sit on your workbench and puts tools and small pieces and parts at your fingertips. (Photo courtesy of Emplast®.)

Another portable option is the two-sided parts case shown in Figure 8.10, which features up to 18 compartments that are totally adjustable, with the provided dividers on one side and three large compartments on the other. Available at home improvement stores and online at www.organize-everything.com, this case is priced at $15.

FIGURE 8.9

This clear plastic box can be transported anywhere so that you have the parts you need, when you need them. (Photo courtesy of Organize-Everything.com.)

FIGURE 8.10
Keep everything sorted and accessible in this two-sided parts case with a sturdy handle for easy transport. (Photo courtesy of Organize-Everything.com.)

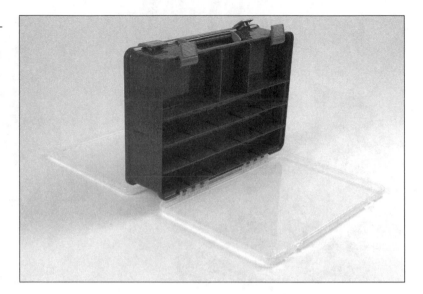

Summary

With all your nuts, bolts, nails, screws, and other small pieces and parts sorted and stored, your entire workbench area should now be organized. Doesn't it look great? Even more importantly, doesn't it feel great? By now, you have hopefully begun to embrace the basic organizing principles and have become an old pro at this. It's all downhill now, as you turn to the next chapter and start to deal with your sporting equipment.

Storing Your Sports Gear

Whether they are old or young, rich or poor, have children and grandchildren or not, people love to engage in sports of one kind or another and are challenged with storing the equipment that goes with it. Although hockey definitely requires more physical activity than golf, both require the purchase of gear and equipment. A person who plays croquet needs a croquet set, an avid camper undoubtedly has boxes upon boxes of camping gear, and a hunter will have guns, ammunition, and a wardrobe of camouflage clothing.

The fact is that most people have varying degrees of sporting goods lurking in their garage. Whether it is all currently being used or will ever be used again is quite another matter. If you want to have an organized garage, all this stuff needs to be organized as well. In this chapter, the organizing principles you learned in Chapter 2, "Understanding the Organizing Process," will be applied to your collection of sporting goods; therefore, if you haven't read it already, I highly recommend you do so. From fishing and fencing to rowing and rollerblading, you will learn the best methods of storing the paraphernalia that goes along with these activities and the available storage systems specifically designed to accommodate these kinds of items.

If you truly don't have any sports gear, you can skip this chapter and begin following the advice in Chapter 10, "Weeding Out Lawn and Garden Clutter," for organizing your lawn and garden supplies.

However, you might want to flip through the pictures anyway, because they should give you helpful suggestions and trigger some good ideas for storing other hard-to-store items in your garage.

To do list

- ☐ Gather up your sports gear and quickly clear out the things you know you don't need or want to keep.
- ☐ Clear the current storage area.
- ☐ Sort and group like items together.
- ☐ Sell or give away the equipment you no longer use.

Organizing Your Sporting Goods

For many of you, organizing your sporting equipment is going to be much easier than organizing other storage centers of the garage. The reason is that most of you do not have the quantity of sports gear as you do tools or lawn and garden items. However, if your garage is beginning to resemble your local sporting goods store, you will need to pay particular attention to the advice in this chapter.

Before you pick up one basketball or tennis racket, I would like you to pause for a moment and list on a piece of paper the sports you and the members of your family currently play. Not the sports you used to play or would play if you had more free time or plan to play five years from now. I am talking about the sports you, your significant other, or children are presently engaged in on a frequent basis or when weather permits. It is important that you be honest with yourself because this will have a significant impact on how you approach the organizing process and how much of this stuff you ultimately decide to keep and store. If you or any other member of your family is no longer playing a sport and have no plans to, then what is the sense of holding on to the gear that goes with it?

Things You'll Need

- ☐ Paper and pen
- ☐ Boxes for sorting things to keep, donate, and sell
- ☐ Trash can
- ☐ Clear space on garage floor or driveway for sorting

Step 1: Reduce the Quantity

When organizing sports gear, a "gross sort" makes a lot of sense. Remember, this is the part of the process when you make the quick-and-easy decisions first that take very little thought at all. If you haven't played baseball in five years, it should be an easy decision to part with your baseball bat and glove, right? Or if the tires on your bicycle have been flat for the past three years, you haven't ridden it in five, and are tired of moving it around to get to everything else, now is time to donate or sell your bike. These kinds of decisions should create little anxiety, speed your progress, and give your spirits a quick lift.

When was the last time you went camping? Right now, you might be looking at all your camping gear and thinking that you need an entire cabinet to hold all the lanterns, cooking stoves and equipment, backpacks, and the rest of the paraphernalia, including sleeping bags, tents, and old blankets. But the reality is that you haven't camped since the kids were in middle school—they are in college now—and your wife never really liked going anyway, but only went to appease you. Get the picture? You are clinging to some fond memories by holding on to this stuff. Yet upon closer inspection, you would likely find that the sleeping bags and tents have begun to mold, deteriorate, and smell so bad that no one would want to sleep in them anyway! The bottom line is that you will still have your memories if you get rid of the stuff.

Step 2: Empty the Storage Area

With your gross sort behind you, you are almost ready to tackle and organize the rest of your sporting equipment. But before you do, it is best to remove everything from the space or container you have designated to store what you will keep. You also need to gather up all the sports gear you can find anywhere else and lay it all out on the garage floor or driveway for sorting. This will give you a more realistic sense of the quantity that remains and will help you better decide how much you can keep and have room for.

Step 3: Sort and Group

Now the fun begins as you continue in your quest to decide what to keep and what to get rid of. Before you can intelligently do that, you need to sort everything by type and determine how many of a particular item you have. When sorting sporting goods, you will first want to group the gear according to the type of sport. You won't know that you have four bicycle tire pumps and seven tennis rackets, three of which need to be restrung or given away, until you gather everything up and begin to group it by sport.

Depending on the quantity of sporting goods you have and the storage systems you select, once your sports gear is sorted by sport, you might ultimately decide to store all the items of a particular type together rather than by individual sport because it is easier and saves space. For some of you, it will make perfect sense to store basketballs, volleyballs, kick balls, and footballs together in the same rack or container, even though they are used in different sports. Others might find it convenient to store baseball bats, hockey sticks, and boat oars together because they are all long and narrow and will fit in one container. The important thing is that you have a system that makes sense to you and that you can find items quickly and easily when you need them.

Step 4: Say Good-bye to What You No Longer Use

Once you have sorted all your family's sports gear, it will be much easier to make rational decisions about what to keep and what to get rid of. Have a trashcan handy, as well as boxes labeled "Donate" and "Garage Sale," for the items you no longer want or need. Some of you will have made these decisions as you sorted; others will struggle with this part of the process and require a few guidelines.

You know that you don't need it all, but it's tough to let go. So, how do you decide what to keep, what to donate, and what to toss? If an item is broken or worn out, toss it because it isn't safe. If it doesn't fit or you haven't used it in the last year or two, give it away or sell it.

If you are still having trouble deciding what to keep and what to part with, ask yourself these questions:

note Even if you don't plan to get rid of anything, sorting your sports gear by sport will make organizing, storing, and finding it so much easier. Then, when you want to go rollerblading, your skates, knee pads, and helmet will all be in one place and you don't have to waste time and energy scavenging through the entire garage to find everything you need. How nice would it be, when you are ready to load your golf clubs in the car for a weekend golf outing, that your golf shoes and the new balls you just bought were stored right beside them? If everything for a particular sport is stored in one place, you can just grab it all and go.

caution Sporting goods that have been subjected to long-term exposure to the elements, such as humidity and extreme heat or cold, can become ruined and unsafe to use. I learned this lesson the hard way after storing my ski boots in the garage for several years and then taking them on a ski trip. One of the boots cracked in half on my first trek down the mountain, and the results could have been disastrous. If you do not heed my warning and insist on improperly storing items that are susceptible to extreme weather conditions, do so at your own risk and be sure to conduct periodic inspections.

- **Do you have enough room to keep it?**—Let's consider the canoe you bought four years ago. You had the best of intentions. You spend two weeks up at the lake every summer and the kids begged you to get it. All went well the first summer. The kids used it a few times and you even used it to paddle out to the middle of the lake one afternoon and caught a few fish. The next summer, the kids weren't so interested in it, and the following summer, you didn't even bother to take it up to the lake with you. This summer, you aren't even sure you are going to the lake because the kids are in summer school. There it sits taking up valuable space you don't have.

- **When was the last time you used it?**—What about the treadmill taking up your side of the garage? You had the best of intentions and figured that if exercise were convenient, you would definitely commit yourself to it. You did great the first three months, but then winter came and it was just too cold to go out there. Meanwhile, winter is almost here again and you haven't stepped back on it since, yet your car is still parked outside. Why not sell the treadmill or give it to a friend or neighbor who might have room for it indoors and will actually use it? This way, you can pull your car back in the garage!

- **What is the worst thing that will happen if you get rid of it?**—This is my favorite question. This might be your old horseback riding saddle or the weight set and bench press you haven't used in years. If you can live with your answer, by all means, let this stuff go! For more information on options for recycling and donating your unwanted items, be sure to read Chapter 13, "Getting Rid of Stuff."

Everyone has his or her reasons for defying conventional wisdom and holding on to something even when he or she should probably just let it go. You can be sure that I have heard almost every reason known to mankind, but I will rarely urge clients to reconsider their decisions. Only you can truly decide whether something is worth keeping. If you are still reluctant after asking yourself the tough questions and storage space is not an issue, keep the item for a while and reevaluate your decision in six months.

To do list

- ☐ Select the appropriate storage solution for your sporting goods.
- ☐ Purchase and install the system or rack (if applicable).
- ☐ Place your organized sports gear into the storage system.

Selecting a Home to Store Your Sports Gear

With the sorting and elimination process complete, you are now left with the sports equipment you want to keep and need to store. Whether you store it where it originally was or you designate a new home for it will depend on the size of the items and the quantity that remains. It doesn't really matter where you choose, as long as the place you select is logical, convenient, and easy to get to.

Although you might choose to keep some of your smaller sporting equipment and accessory items in well-labeled containers, sorted by sport or by season, you will find that much of this gear is rather large and doesn't lend itself well to being containerized. This is one reason why there are so many different kinds of wall-mount sports racks on the market—to help you get this stuff up off the floor and out of your way. Although hanging is going to be the preferred method of storage for many of these items, drawers will work for smaller items such as elbow and knee pads and swimming and golf accessories, and this will keep them cleaner, too.

Using What You Already Have

Many economical methods of storage are easily transportable and are quite effective in housing all kinds of sports gear. You might already have some of these items around the house and are already using them for this purpose:

- Clean garbage pails work great for storing all kinds of things, including skis, ski poles, bats, hockey sticks, oars, paddles, and just about anything that is long and narrow. They are waterproof and can be used to hold an assortment of balls as well.

- Plastic laundry baskets and milk crates can be placed off the ground on a low shelf and used to store toys, baseball mitts, balls, and other small items. A different one can be designated for each member of the family or a particular sport, by color. Kids love rummaging through them, and it's very easy for

tip The last thing you want is for the kids to bang up your cars as they tote this stuff in and out of the garage. For this reason, you might want to consider storing frequently used items near the garage doors themselves, so this stuff can be more easily transported in and out. For more help in selecting the best home for your sporting goods, you will want to read Chapter 3, "Reviewing Storage Options," and Chapter 4, "Selecting Storage Systems," if you haven't done so already.

caution Give serious consideration before putting any of your sporting goods up in the attic. The old saying, "Out of sight, out of mind," applies here. Unless you are diligent about bringing them down when the appropriate season arrives, you might as well give them away because you are likely to forget that they are up there. There is also the added probability that some items will be ruined by the extreme heat or cold.

them to put their sports gear and toys away. Also, these items are portable for when you go to the park or to visit friends and relatives.

- Old laundry hampers work well for storing balls and bats and other smaller items. Newer rolling laundry hampers with several fabric or mesh compartments work even better. The kids can roll the hamper out when they are playing, and it makes cleaning up so much easier. The steel frame Sort and Store shown in Figure 9.1 is a durable storage center that comes with three removable mesh bags. It is available online at www.stacksandstacks.com.

FIGURE 9.1
The Sort and Store is a simple solution for storing all kinds of sporting goods and makes transporting things a breeze. (Photo courtesy of Stacks and Stacks.)

Storing Bicycles

The one piece of sporting equipment most commonly found in the garage is the bicycle. The problem is that there is usually more than one, and the challenge is to store them out of the way to avoid accidental falls resulting in dents and scratches on your car, but not so out of the way that it becomes cumbersome to access and use them. This is probably the reason why there are more options for storing bicycles than most any other piece of sporting equipment. Bicycles can be securely hung from the ceiling, on the wall or on a pole, or placed in a bike rack.

Until the recent interest in the garage market by product manufacturers and the dawn of a new era of manufactured products, storing bicycles in a bike rack was one of the more widely used options. If you have the space required, few options can beat the easy access of a bike rack. The Grandstand™, shown in Figure 9.2, is priced at $20. It's a lightweight portable option that stores all kinds of bikes. If biking is an activity your whole family engages in and you have adequate space, you should consider the heavy-duty steel bike rack shown in Figure 9.3, which holds six bicycles and all kinds of accessories, too. The unit is easy to assemble and it is available at www.organize-everything.com for just under $150.

One popular, inexpensive storage option for bicycles is to hang them from the ceiling using ladder hooks, though this is not my favorite because getting them down can prove to be a bit unwieldy. It can be so awkward for some that once up there, the bikes are there to stay. Although this is a great option for seasonal storage, if you are planning to use your bicycle frequently, I do not recommend it.

The good news is that there are plenty of other storage options that are very economical. Not only will these methods get your bicycles up off the floor and out of the way, but they will ensure easy access, too. There are many brands of floor-to-ceiling bike racks like the one shown in Figure 9.4, which adjusts from 6' to 11' to fit most areas and sells for around $100 at numerous online retailers as well as at bicycle stores everywhere. The storage hooks adjust to fit most types of bicycles and are vinyl coated to protect your bicycle's finish.

FIGURE 9.4
This floor-to-ceiling rack holds two bicycles, and additional hooks can be added so that it will accommodate four.

If your preference is to hang your bicycle on the wall, you have a number of choices in all price ranges. Racor® products and the lesser expensive ProStor product line (www.racorinc.com) have certainly cornered the sports hook, hanger, and rack market for bicycle storage (and storage for other types of sporting goods as well). The company manufactures several styles of wall-mount racks that range in price from $18 to $75 and allow you to store up to two bicycles at once, flat against the wall. Some of them even come with a shelf to store helmets and other biking accessories. These products are widely available in retail stores and from numerous online retailers, including www.stacksandstacks.com.

tip
Store your bicycle helmet on the seat of the bike or attached to the handle bars. Not only does this keep it handy and convenient, but it reminds you to use it!

Barry's Best

The ProStor Iron Wedge bike hook, shown in Figure 9.5, can be mounted on the wall or ceiling and allows you to hang your bike by the wheel in a cushioned sleeve to prevent damage. This steel hook comes with a lifetime warranty and can be used to hang many other items in the garage as well.

Hanging bicycles from the wall or ceiling is easy with ProStor's Iron Wedge. (Photo courtesy of Stacks and Stacks.)

If you truly want to get your bicycle up and out of the way, you might consider a product like the ProStor Hoist Monster, shown in Figure 9.6. This steel system will raise up to 50 pounds with ease, and accidental release is prevented with a special rope-locking mechanism. The Hoist Monster requires no assembly and is available at a wide variety of retail stores and online at www.organize-everything.com for less than $50.

Hoist your bicycle up, up, and safely away to ceilings up to 14' high. (Photo courtesy of Racor®.)

Storing Balls and Children's Toys

For the majority of sports, usually a ball of some sort is involved. Balls can be troublesome to store and are easily lost because, except for the football, all of them are round and they come in a wide range of sizes. But actually, balls can be stored quite simply and very inexpensively. Each type of ball can be stored with the rest of the gear from that particular sport, or you might choose to store all the balls together in one place. Either way works well, and one isn't preferable over the other. Your decision will ultimately depend on the quantity you have and what works best for you.

If you are going to store all the balls together, the simplest and most economical way to do it is to use a clean garbage pail, milk crate, or laundry basket. If you want to get fancier, many other kinds of holders are specially made for this purpose, such as the rolling wire mesh unit shown in Figure 9.7, manufactured by Rubbermaid.

FIGURE 9.7

This is one of the many types of products available to make storing balls simple and easy. (Photo courtesy of Rubbermaid.)

In addition to balls, children have all kinds of sports gear and toys that need to be stored. Think about hanging items such as hula hoops and jump ropes, but just remember to hang them low enough so that children can reach them. Beach and swimming pool toys can be hung on the wall in a deep basket or in a mesh bag that you can just throw in the back of your car when you are headed to the public swimming pool.

From Frisbees and squirt guns to trucks and kiddy toolsets, the StoreWALL™ system, shown in Figure 9.8, offers a variety of hooks, baskets, and shelves that not only can accommodate balls, but a host of other items as well. See Chapter 4 for more information about StoreWALL™, or visit its website at www.storewall.com.

FIGURE 9.8
This wall-mount system includes all the accessories needed to store balls and a wide variety of children's toys. (Photo courtesy of StoreWALL™.)

BASIC BATTERY STORAGE

As most parents well know, many popular children's toys require batteries. Nothing is worse than not having the right size battery when the old ones wear out—except perhaps knowing that you have some and not being able to find them! The deluxe Battery Rack Emergency Center, shown here, is available for less than $30 from www.organize-everything.com. Battery racks that mount on the wall or fit inside a drawer are available without all the bells and whistles for about half that price.

The Battery Rack Emergency Center not only holds all your batteries, but also features a clock, ready-to-go flashlight, and an AM/FM radio that you can play while you are out in the garage.

One unique accessory designed especially for children (but adults love it, too) is the Kid'z sports locker, shown in Figure 9.9, by the makers of the GarageTek® system. Every member of the family can have his or her own locker for storing personal gear. The lockers feature an adjustable shelf and are available in two colors: blue and purple. To learn more about the GarageTek® system, see Chapter 4 or visit www.garagetek.com.

FIGURE 9.9
Everyone in this family is happy. The kids love having their own locker to store their stuff, and Mom and Dad like the fact that it is no longer lying all over the garage floor. (Photo courtesy of GarageTek®.)

Specialty Racks for Specific Sports

Product manufacturers have been quick to create products that meet the needs of people with active lifestyles and interests. Numerous specialty racks are available to appease the aficionado of practically any sport. Let's look at some of the racks available for various activities.

Fishing is a favorite American pastime for many, and the people at Racor® have designed a solid steel rack, shown in Figure 9.10, that holds up to six fishing rods. It sells for less than $40 and is available at a wide variety of retail and online stores, such as www.stacksandstacks.com.

FIGURE 9.10
Your fishing rods are safely stored in this rack, which mounts easily to the wall and has a lifetime warranty. (Photo courtesy of Racor®.)

STORING CANOES AND KAYAKS, PADDLES AND OARS

Storing canoes, kayaks, and the gear associated with these water sports is easy if your garage has open rafters. Just straddle these items across the rafters to get them up and out of the way. If you are not lucky enough to have open rafters, visit www.rackwarehouse.com to order the unique JEMB Watersport Hanging Storage System pictured here. This polypropylene hanging storage rack holds up to three kayaks, with a 200-pound capacity, and is available for less than $50. You can use mop and broom clips attached to the wall to stow oars and paddles. Hang lifejackets so they thoroughly dry out and are out of the way, or store them on a high shelf or loft.

This easy-to-install rack holds kayaks, windsurfers, and paddles. (Photo courtesy of The Rack Warehouse.)

For all you golf enthusiasts, take a look at the floor-supported golf organizer, shown in Figure 9.11, with adjustable legs for easy leveling. It holds two golf bags and all your golfing accessories. You can store loose balls and tees in the open bin on top. It is available for $60 from national home product retailers such as Bed Bath & Beyond® and Linens 'n Things or online at www.stacksandstacks.com.

Whether you are a cross-country or downhill skier, the steel Racor® ski rack shown in Figure 9.12 will hold up to four pairs of skis and the poles to go with them.

tip Get an inexpensive shoe rack and keep it in the garage to store all those golf, bowling, baseball, tennis, hiking, and jogging shoes.

FIGURE 9.11
This easy-to-assemble golf organizer holds two bags of clubs and your golf shoes, balls, and tees. (Photo courtesy of Stacks and Stacks.)

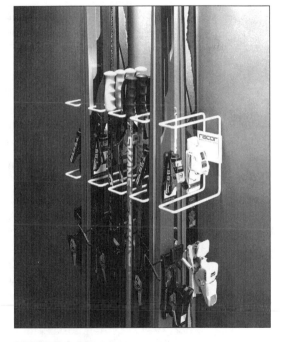

FIGURE 9.12
This ski rack requires no assembly, mounts easily to the wall, and has a lifetime warranty. (Photo courtesy of Racor®.)

Combo Sports Racks

The Sports Gear Rack by GarageTek®, shown in Figure 9.13, holds up to 30 pounds of sports equipment. You name it, the Sports Gear Rack holds it...and gets it up and out of the way.

FIGURE 9.13
This rack mounts on the wall and can store just about any sports item you can imagine. (Photo courtesy of GarageTek®.)

The Rubbermaid multisport rack shown in Figure 9.14 holds anything from balls and bats to helmets and hockey sticks, and it sports a removable mesh bag. The unit resists moisture and will not warp, crack, rust, or rot. It is available at home improvement stores and discount superstores nationwide.

The heavy-duty steel sports rack shown in Figure 9.15 is built to last and is designed to hold just about anything. The lower shelf is ideal for storing skates, bowling balls, and larger items, and the top shelf is ideal for balls and smaller items. It is easy to assemble and includes hooks for hanging and a special rack to hold up to three baseball bats. This steel sports rack is available online at www.stacksandstacks for less than $100.

Complete Sports Storage Systems

There isn't much of anything that you can't store on the Elfa® system shown in Figure 9.16, but it's designed especially to store a variety of sporting goods. This system includes special bracket posts for ski storage, utility hooks for rackets and hockey sticks, shelf baskets for balls and skates, a hook rail for baseball gear, and side hooks, too, which are ideal for hanging all sorts of things, including golf clubs. See Chapter 4 for complete information on the Elfa® system, or visit www.thecontainerstore.com.

Schulte® has created a complete line of unique hooks and racks for virtually every sport imaginable. It can be attached directly to the wall, to the Schulte® steel Activity Organizer Grid system, to Schulte® slotwall, and to StoreWALL™ and other slatwall systems. The system shown in Figure 9.17 illustrates that with careful planning, you can organize one wall to serve virtually all your storage needs for sporting goods and related accessories. For more information on Schulte® products, see Chapter 4 or visit www.schultestorage.com. The products are sold at Organized Living stores and at www.organize-everything.com.

FIGURE 9.15
This utility sports rack comes equipped with locking wheels for total mobility and performance exactly where you need it. (Photo courtesy of Stacks and Stacks.)

FIGURE 9.14
This combo rack will store sports gear for the entire family. (Photo courtesy of Rubbermaid.)

FIGURE 9.16
The Elfa® garage storage system is totally adjustable. As your needs change, so can your system. (Photo courtesy of The Container Store.)

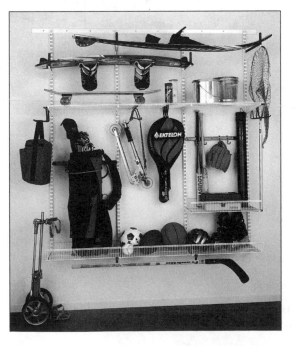

FIGURE 9.17
No matter what the sport, the people at Schulte® have created a way for you to store it. (Photo courtesy of Schulte®.)

FIGURE 9.17 No matter what the sport, the people at Schulte® have created a way for you to store it. (Photo courtesy of Schulte®.)

Summary

Well that wasn't so bad, was it? You can breathe a big sigh of relief with all your sports gear safely stowed and out of the way. No more tripping over bicycles to get from the house to the car, and it is so nice to see all your sporting gear in one place so that you really can find what you need when you are ready to use it. Pat yourself on the back and reward yourself with 9 holes of golf or an evening of rollerblading around the park. Just don't forget to put everything back in its new home when you return. Then, when you're ready, start reading the next chapter, where we will apply all the principles you have already learned to weed out your lawn and garden supplies. The end is in sight, so stick with it!

Weeding Out Lawn and Garden Clutter

10

Most homeowners take enormous pride in their manicured gardens and well-kept lawns. Although we want our property to look pristine at all times, many of us are too busy to perform the necessary maintenance ourselves and have relegated it to a lawn service. Others of us refuse to give up the opportunity to commune with the land and continue to perform all these tasks ourselves. For many, lawn work is good therapy.

Regardless of which category you fall into, it is almost certain your garage has become a graveyard of the lawn and garden equipment you have accumulated over the years that is broken, worn out, or no longer used—blown-out leaf blowers, cracked terra cotta pots, and lifeless lawnmowers. The rest of you have accumulated so much that despite the fact you have more than one duplicate of everything, you still can't find your hoe when you need it.

The organizing principles you will use to organize your lawn and garden equipment are the same as those outlined in Chapter 2, "Understanding the Organizing Process," and that we have used throughout this book to organize other storage centers in the garage. Not only will you be guided through the organizing process in this chapter, but you will learn the best method for storing all the lawn and garden equipment you need.

In this chapter:

* Sorting and organizing lawn and garden items
* Determining which items to keep
* Assessing appropriate storage methods
* Storing wheelbarrows and other bulky items
* Choosing the storage system that's right for you

If you have a lawn service and have already gotten rid of most of this stuff, you can proceed to Chapter 11, "Stashing Seasonal Stuff," and learn how to properly store your seasonal items.

To do list

- ☐ Make quick-and-easy decisions about what to get rid of first.
- ☐ Clear the current storage area.
- ☐ Sort and group like things together.
- ☐ Eliminate items you no longer use.
- ☐ Choose the system that is right for you.
- ☐ Place items in their new home.

Organizing Tools and Other Lawn and Garden Items

One would think that the amount of lawn and garden tools and supplies that people have would depend on the amount of work they do in the yard, but this is not the case. Even when people decide to hire a lawn-cutting service or a gardener, they are reluctant to get rid of the tools… just in case. Actually, this makes sense, and I would not advocate that the moment you decide to hire a lawn-care service that you immediately sell your lawnmowers, the edger, the blower, and everything else—although that was the first thing I did! It makes good sense to hold on to these things for a while in case you change your mind later or until you are sure your days of mowing the lawn and mulching the garden are behind you forever.

Unless you have lots of free time on your hands, I find that once you get used to the idea of paying a service to perform lawn maintenance on a routine basis, you get pretty spoiled and rarely do you have a change of heart. It's nice to have all those summer weekends free instead of being obligated to push a lawnmower, though it is great exercise. And I don't know about you, but there are lots of other things I would rather be doing on autumn afternoons than raking leaves.

Before you begin to sort and organize your lawn and garden items, you need to assess whether you plan to do the lawn work yourself or hire another company to do it. If you are intent on continuing to do it yourself, you will need more of the equipment than someone who uses a lawn-care service and would not consider doing this work again themselves.

Things You'll Need

- ☐ Boxes for sorting things to keep, donate, and sell
- ☐ Trash can
- ☐ Clear space on garage floor or driveway for sorting

Step 1: Reduce the Quantity

This is the easy part of the organizing process where you make the simplest and easiest decisions first. Take a quick look around and begin with the larger equipment. If you are no longer cutting your grass and have no intention of doing so again, you no longer need a riding lawnmower and two push models, right? You might choose to keep one, just in case, but you certainly don't need three.

Do you still need a gasoline-powered edger, if you have a weed wacker? Your hedge trimmer is a beauty and has hardly been used, but the house you are currently living in doesn't have any bushes! What are you holding onto it for? And what about all those pieces and parts that belonged to your sprinkler system from your last house? You have been in your new house for three years now and you still haven't had a sprinkler system installed. Do you think you still need them?

Okay, you get the idea. Look around and pick out the things you can easily decide that you no longer need. Don't agonize over it, and focus on setting aside just those items whose loss will cause you little or no anxiety. You will be surprised how easy this is as you start looking at all the stuff you haven't touched in years. If you have been carting that pitchfork around in the last three moves and have never once used it, or come across 50 plastic flower pots and have no idea why you are saving them, get rid of them now as the first step of the organizing process.

Step 2: Clear the Storage Area

In preparation for further sorting, you will need to remove all lawn and garden items from the areas where they are presently being stored. Some of you are storing these things in the garage and the remainder in an outdoor shed, whether by design or as a result of overaccumulation. When the garage was full, you bought a shed and started putting the overflow out there.

It is essential that you gather everything up so you can see what and how much you have. You have forgotten about half the things stored out in the shed or buried deep within your garage. Until you lay everything out and begin sorting, you won't know what the best storage location will be. You might very well return everything to its original location or choose a more convenient one.

Step 3: Sort and Group

You will begin the sorting process by grouping your lawn and garden equipment into these major categories: power equipment (lawnmowers, weed wackers, blowers, trimmers), large long-handled tools (rakes, shovels, brooms), gardening items (small hand tools, flower pots, liquid and granular fertilizers), irrigation equipment, and so on. This will help you determine how many or much of a particular item you have and is an integral step that will speed up the weeding and elimination process.

> **tip** Because lawn and garden items tend to be so large, you will find that the garage floor or the driveway works well for a sorting area.

When things are sorted and stored with other similar items, it's so much easier to find the things you want when you need them. Once the items have been grouped by category, select the category with the largest items and begin by sorting those items first and working your way through to the smaller ones. You will make speedier progress and get less bogged down in the process.

It is during the sorting process when you will discover that you actually own six shovels, though you could have sworn you were down to your last one and had wondered where the other five had disappeared to. Or you'll learn that you really didn't need to buy that new leaf blower after all, because you already had one out in the shed, but it was buried under a mildewed moving blanket.

Step 4: Weed and Purge

For some, the weeding and purging process is connected to the sorting process, and others will view it as a separate component. It really doesn't matter, as long as you do it. But for many, this is the hardest part of the process because it is so easy to think of reasons why you should hold on to something just for a little while longer. After all, you paid good money for it and you have hardly ever used it. However, the real question is, *will* you ever use it? Yes, you really might need it someday, but if you are reluctant to give up your snow blower and you live in Dallas, Texas, hopefully you can see what's wrong with that picture.

Here is a quick recap of the critical questions discussed in Chapter 2 that will guide you in making the more difficult decisions:

- When was the last time you used it or have you ever used it? Can you rationalize keeping two lawnmowers now that you have hired a lawn-care service? Are you ever going to hang that hammock up in the backyard that has been in a box since Father's Day four years ago?

- Is the item in good working condition and safe to keep? Think about how much it will cost. Is it even worth repairing your broken weed wacker? More than likely, you could purchase a new one for less money. If an item can't be fixed, why would you want to hold on to it?

- Is it something that is still relevant and useful? Are the weather-beaten cushions from your last set of lawn furniture worth holding on to?

- Do you have a logical place and enough space to keep it? I can understand that it would be nice to keep your riding lawnmower, even though the lawn of your current home is much smaller than the last one, but your garage is smaller too, and where do you plan to store it?

- What is the worst thing that will happen if you get rid of it? Is your world going to stop spinning? I doubt it, and in most cases, not only will you be able to live with your answer, but you'll have no trouble utilizing the new-found space.

Step 5: Putting Things Back

Now that you have completed the sorting process and have decided what you can and can't live without, you need to decide the best method of storage for these things before you can put them back. For a complete review of storage options, see Chapter 3 if you haven't read it already.

Of all the storage methods available for lawn and garden equipment, you will find that hanging is by far the most practical method for lots of these items. Many commonly used items such as rakes, shovels, and brooms are bulky and have long, thick handles, so hanging makes good sense. It gets them off the floor and out of the way. In addition to the many quick, easy, and economical hanging options mentioned in Chapter 3, the wall-mount hanging rack shown in Figure 10.1 is just one of many types available that are inexpensive, easily installed, and widely available at home improvement and discount stores everywhere.

The Space Logic™ soft-side Extra Tall Organizer, shown in Figure 10.2, is manufactured by Case Logic and mounts just about anywhere. The heavy-duty construction sports two tear-resistant zippered compartments and a reinforced bottom to hold extra-heavy items. It is available for less than $30 at Target, ShopKo, and Fred Meyer stores nationwide, as well as online at www.stacksandstacks.com.

The Schulte® Grid system shown in Figure 10.3 is available in 2'×4' sections made of heavy-gauge epoxy-coated steel and can be mounted horizontally or vertically. With a variety of hooks and baskets manufactured to fit the grid or to mount directly to the wall, you can hang anything from ladders and rakes to hoses and hedge trimmers with ease.

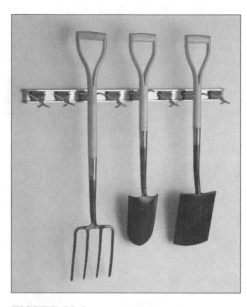

FIGURE 10.1
This standard hanging rack holds any size handle firmly in place. (Photo courtesy of Container Store.)

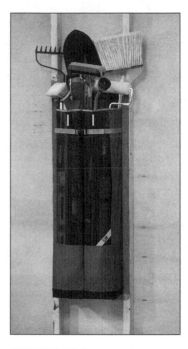

FIGURE 10.2
This soft-sided organizer mounts in minutes and features a tension strap to hold items securely inside the see-through pockets. (Photo courtesy of Case Logic.)

FIGURE 10.3
Hooks and baskets simply snap into this grid (without tools) to store a wide variety of lawn and garden products. (Photo courtesy of Schulte®.)

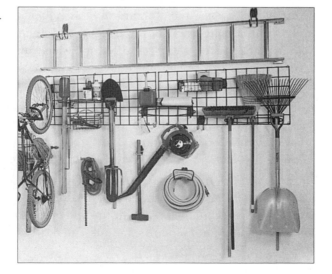

STORING YOUR WHEELBARROW

Wheelbarrows are great when you need them, but most definitely a challenge to store the rest of the time. They are heavy, cumbersome, and take up a lot of space when stored on the floor. Until someone develops a collapsible version, one of the best things I have found is a specially designed two-piece wheelbarrow holder bracket available for less than $5 at Home Depot. The front lip of the wheelbarrow sits in the bottom bracket and the other end snaps into the top bracket. In seconds, your wheelbarrow is up off the floor and out of your way.

Some lawn and garden items are not suitable for hanging, and they store much better in a drawer or in a container placed on a shelf. Sprinkler heads and other lose pieces and parts pertaining to your irrigation system are ideal candidates to be stored in this manner. Depending on the size of the drawer and the quantity of items being stored in it, you can partition the drawer into sections or containerize the items within it to keep them sorted, as shown in Figure 10.4.

FIGURE 10.4
A drawer is an ideal solution for storing small pieces and parts to keep them organized and together.

Creating a Suitable Storage System

Because lawn and garden equipment can be so large and bulky, not to mention dirty, you might have little choice but to continue storing it in two places—such as the garage and a shed. After you have completed the sorting and elimination process, if you discover that there isn't enough room to store all your equipment in the garage and still be able to park your cars in there, then using a shed is your best option. If you don't already have one, see Chapter 5, "Analyzing Alternative Storage Solutions," for help on selecting the type of shed that will work best for you.

tip If you like to grow your plants from seed, there are several great ways to store your collection of flower and vegetable seed packets. You can store them in a drawer, in a 3"×5" index card box (alphabetically if you wish), or slip them in the pockets of see-through loose-leaf pages designed for base-ball cards.

Economical Methods of Storage

You probably have a number of things around your house that you never thought of using to help store your lawn and garden items. If you enjoy working in the garden, you know how important it is to keep your small garden tools together so you can just grab them and have what you need at your fingertips. A small bucket or a plastic double-sided cleaning caddy works great for this purpose, and you can hose it off when it gets dirty. You can buy a gardener's belt at discount and home improvement stores for less than $10.

Use a clean garbage pail to store brooms, rakes, shovels, and other items with long handles. It keeps them together and makes it easy to grab what you need. Just be sure to put a heavy weight or bricks at the bottom so it won't tip over. If you use a garbage container that has wheels, you can wheel everything right out to the garden and save a lot of running back and forth to the garage. And if you have an old golf bag standing around that you are no longer using, you can attach it to the wall and store these long-handled items in it as well.

tip Don't throw away your old throw rugs no matter how awful they look. These tattered eyesores make great kneeling pads for you to save your knees when working in the garden.

Start collecting a few five-gallon buckets with lids from friends or any painters you know, or you can collect those large plastic buckets of kitty litter or containers from warehouse stores that hold bulk sizes of food. As shown in Figure 10.5, these are all excellent no-cost options for storing all kinds of things, such as potting soil, bird seed, fertilizers, and grass seed, just to name a few. What's more, they will keep rodents and bugs out as well. Of course, make sure they are well labeled because you are likely to forget what is in them, especially if they are all the same size and color.

FIGURE 10.5
These containers keep your fertilizers, seeds, and so on dry, clean, and free of rodents and pests. Label containers so you know what's stored within them.

Another very affordable option for the storage of rakes, brooms, and shovels is the floor-supported Rubbermaid® tool caddies, which come in two different shapes and sizes, as shown in Figure 10.6. Both are very affordable, assemble easily in minutes, and won't crack, rust, rot, or warp. The Tool Tower holds more than 36 lawn and garden tools and has a special slot for a weed wacker, blower, or edger. The Corner Rack holds up to 30 tools and eliminates wasted corner space. Both are available at discount stores everywhere.

caution

When possible, store fertilizers, plant food, herbicides, and other toxic substances in a locked cabinet or on a high shelf. This is especially important when young children will have access to them.

Complete Storage Systems for Less Than $500

With a bit of ingenuity, it is amazing what a great system you can put together without stretching your wallet. The ClosetMaid® system, shown in Figure 10.7, is a collection of affordable wall-mount shelves, racks, and hooks to hold the majority of your lawn and garden needs. The items pictured are easily installed and are available at home improvement centers nationwide. The gardening tools organizer by Stacks and Stacks (www.stacksandstacks.com), shown in Figure 10.8, is sold as a kit that comes with the necessary shelves, baskets, and hooks to create a basic gardening center.

FIGURE 10.6
For a quick-and-easy
solution for lawn and
garden tool storage,
you can't beat these
Rubbermaid® prod-
ucts for quality or
price. (Photo courtesy
of Rubbermaid®.)

FIGURE 10.7
With these inexpen-
sive components to
choose from, it is easy
to create the system
that is just right for
you. (Photo courtesy
of ClosetMaid®.)

FIGURE 10.8
If gardening is your passion, this wall-mount kit puts everything within easy reach. (Photo courtesy of Stacks and Stacks.)

An outstanding value in this price category is the FastTrack® system by Rubbermaid®, as shown in Figure 10.9. With more than a dozen accessories and hooks that hold up to 50 pounds, you can hang virtually any lawn and garden item from the rail, which features a stylish PVC cover, and move things around as often as you wish. The system is available at Menard's and Bed Bath & Beyond®, and you can outfit an entire wall for around $250.

tip When stacking flower pots of the same size inside each other, you can use a plastic bag between them for cushioning and to make it easier to get them apart later.

FIGURE 10.9
You can hang just about any lawn and garden item you can think of from Rubbermaid's FastTrack® system, including a wheelbarrow. (Photo courtesy of Rubbermaid®.)

Complete Storage Systems for More Than $500

The StoreWALL™ slatwall system, shown in Figure 10.10, provides an unlimited number of options for storing lawn and garden tools and equipment. The easy-to-install PVC panels are available in five colors and won't crack or splinter. The system accommodates a multitude of hooks, racks, and baskets manufactured by Schulte®. StoreWALL™ products are available through closet companies, garage storage dealers, and installers found on the company's website (www.storewall.com), or they can be ordered by mail from Storic Storage Systems at www.storic.com.

There isn't anything that the Whirlpool Corporation has not thought of in designing the Gladiator™ Garage Works system. You can mix and match the high-tech modular units, cabinetry, and appliances with powder-coated steel fronts and choose between two hanging options—Gear Wall™ panels or Gear Track™ panels—to create a gardener's paradise (see Figure 10.11). The systems are sold at Lowe's and Sears, or you can find a dealer in your area by visiting the Gladiator™ website (www.gladiatorgw.com).

FIGURE 10.10
With its high load capacity, The StoreWALL™ system is strong enough to hang all kinds of things. (Photo courtesy of Garage Interiors of Michigan.)

FIGURE 10.11
The Gladiator™ system comes with a 10-year-to-lifetime limited warranty and will make your garage the envy of the neighborhood. (Photo courtesy of Gladiator™ by Whirlpool.)

Summary

Were you surprised at how quickly you were able to wade through all that stuff? You shouldn't be, because once you learn the basic organizing principles, it's so easy to apply them to just about anything you want to organize. I wish I could be there to see that big smile on your face and congratulate you personally.

Are you beginning to see the light flickering at the end of the tunnel? You should, because now that you have weeded through and organized all your lawn and garden tools and supplies, your garage-organizing project is almost complete. The only major things left to organize are your holiday decorations and other seasonal items, which will be covered in the next chapter. If you don't have any seasonal items to store, you can skip Chapter 11 and move on to Part III, "Beyond the Basics," where you will learn how to clean and protect the garage floor and various options for getting rid of all the stuff you have purged throughout this project.

Stashing Seasonal Stuff

Most of us store seasonal items of one sort or another. From patio furniture and pool paraphernalia to holiday decorations and snow-removal equipment, this can be some of the trickiest stuff to store. Not only are many of these items bulky and take up a lot of storage space, they aren't used year round, which makes it even more challenging to have them accessible when you need them and out of the way when you don't.

Of course, the exact items that are considered seasonal and the type and quantity of what you have will vary depending on the climate where you live. If you live up north, it will be more challenging to find a place for your spring and summer items because you have so much winter equipment and gear that you need to keep on hand. Whereas if you live in the southern warmer climates, you will probably have lots of patio, pool, and lawn gear that you use throughout the year and your need for a snow blower or snow shovel is virtually nonexistent.

In this chapter, after a quick review of the organizing principles discussed in Chapter 2, "Understanding the Organizing Process," you will learn unique storage solutions and tips to accommodate the holiday decorations and seasonal items you need. With good storage systems in place, you can more easily access these items when you need them.

To do list

- ☐ Gather up your seasonal items and clear current storage areas.
- ☐ Sort and group like items together.
- ☐ Select a home and put items back.

Organizing Seasonal Items

Whether you are organizing holiday decorations or winter necessities, the basic principles are the same. If you have just started this project, you should consider reading Chapter 2 before you proceed. However, if you have worked through this book chapter by chapter and have almost finished organizing your entire garage, you are already an old pro at this and could probably teach me a thing or two. Assuming that you are somewhere in between, here is a quick recap of the steps you should follow to effectively organize your collection of seasonal items.

Things You'll Need

- ☐ Boxes for sorting things to keep, donate, and sell
- ☐ Trash can
- ☐ Clear space on workbench, table, or garage floor for sorting

Step 1: Reduce the Quantity

Where is your winter snow-removal equipment? Is part of it out in the shed and part of it in the garage? What about the pool equipment? Are some of your patio furniture cushions being stored in the attic and the rest of them out in the shed, or did you buy a new set last spring because you couldn't remember where you stored the set you bought the year before?

Before you can realistically sort and organize your seasonal items, you need to gather them up and see how much there is. Because you don't use these things year-round, it's easy to forget what you have. How can you organize your holiday decorations if part of them are in the hall closet behind the coats, some are out in the garage, and the rest are up in the attic? You won't know that you have three snow shovels or five Christmas tree toppers until you collect everything in one place and inventory it.

Once everything is in one place, it is time to
make the easy decisions that require very little
thought of what you can live without. For example, if you moved from Denver to Miami, why on
earth do you still have a snow shovel and tire
chains? Or do you really still need your picnic
table umbrella, even though you no longer have
a picnic table? Quickly separate the things you
know you don't want or need, and move on.

> **tip** If you have to ponder about any item for more than 15 seconds, put it aside and keep going. You don't want to lose your momentum, and you can always make the decision to get rid of it later.

Step 2: Empty the Storage Area

If you have not already done so, remove all seasonal items from the areas where
they are currently being stored. Whether you are storing them in the attic, a loft, on
shelves in the garage, or out in the shed, you need to lay everything out and see
what you have. Once you do this, you can begin the sorting process, and you will
get a better idea of how much you can keep and what you have room for. By the
time you finish the sorting process, you might very well want to reevaluate where
you want to store this stuff anyway.

Step 3: Sort and Group

Because there are so many different kinds of seasonal items, you will first begin sorting the items
into major categories: patio furniture and accessories, lawn and beach chairs, outdoor party supplies, snow-removal equipment, holiday decorations,

> **note** For specific sorting guide-lines, refer to Chapter 2, "Understanding the Organizing Process."

and so forth. Once items have been sorted into major categories, you will then need
to sort within each category. For example, once your holiday decorations are all in
one place, you will begin to sort them by holiday: Christmas, Hanukkah, Halloween,
Easter, and so on.

For some of you, the sorting process will go very quickly because you will have very
little in any of these categories, whereas others will have much more and need to
spend a lot more time on this part. Take whatever time you need to sort things thoroughly. Not only will this speed up the elimination portion of the process, but it will
be a big help in determining how and where you will store everything when you are
ready to put things back.

Step 4: Deciding to Get Rid of Things You Don't Need

Now that your seasonal items are well sorted within each category, it will be much
easier for you to decide what you can get rid of and what you need to keep. I am

sure that some of you will have already tossed or put things aside to be donated as part of the sorting process (you learn more about how to recycle, sell, donate, and otherwise dispose of unwanted items in Chapter 13, "Getting Rid of Stuff"). But for those of you who didn't, use the following questions as a guide, and you will be amazed how fast they can help you race through the process:

- When was the last time you used it or have you ever used it? Now that you have moved to a condo and the association is responsible for all the snow removal, do you really need three snow shovels? I can understand wanting to keep one to be able to shovel off your own steps perhaps, but three? If you have four sets of tree ornaments and haven't used one set for the last five years, why don't you just give it away?

- Is the item in good working condition and safe to keep? If you have any doubt about the safety of the Christmas tree lights you are using or the rotating color wheel that shines on your tree, throw them out and get new ones. They aren't worth repairing and certainly not worth risking a fire.

- Is it something that is still relevant and useful? You no longer lay out in the sun and haven't for years. Most of the straps on both of your outdoor lounge chairs are broken and you haven't gotten around to getting them repaired, yet you are still holding on to them. What's wrong with this picture?

- Do you have a logical place and enough space to keep it? I realize that you paid a lot of money for your snowmobile, but you have only used it twice. You promised your son that you would buy a riding lawn mower by next summer if he would cut the grass so you could start playing more golf on the weekends. The problem is that you only have room to store one or the other and still be able to park your cars in the garage. Golf every weekend or a snowmobile that you rarely use—I'll leave the choice up to you.

- What is the worst thing that will happen if you get rid of it? In most cases, nothing. So resist the temptation to hold on to something that you clearly no longer need and give or sell it to someone else who can use it.

As you sort through your seasonal items using these questions to guide you, you will undoubtedly run across lots of items that you decide you can part with. Those items that would be of no use to anyone can be tossed or recycled. Place the remaining items that you plan to give away or sell in boxes labeled "Donate" or "Garage Sale."

Step 5: Putting Things Back

After the sorting and elimination process is completed, it is time to look at what remains and assign a suitable home. Depending on the size and quantity of what remains, you will either return the items to the same place or designate a new home. Rather than repeat the multitude of storage options that exist for storing seasonal items, let me just refer you to Chapter 3, "Reviewing Storage Options," for more information. You will find Table 3.1, "Suitable Storage Options," to be especially helpful, as many of the items listed are seasonal ones.

> **tip**
> Store your screens and storm windows across the exposed beams in ceiling rafters or in a garage loft area. You can store other items in this area, too, by using plywood sheets to create a loft; see Chapter 3 for more information.

If you have limited space in your garage and you also have a shed, consider keeping the things you use most in the winter in the garage and put the summer items you won't need out in the shed. I realize that this is more work, but when it's below freezing outside, it will save you a trip out to the shed and keep the things you need at your fingertips. Then, when the seasons change, you can switch things back.

If you need some additional space for storing seasonal and outdoor items and you don't need or want to purchase a shed or install a loft, consider a deck box, as shown in Figure 11.1. Deck boxes are a great place to store patio furniture cushions or pool supplies, towels, and toys. They come in all shapes and sizes and are available at major home improvement stores and discount retailers.

FIGURE 11.1
This all-weather deck box has 10 cubic feet of storage capacity, and the interlocking panels make it easy to assemble. (Photo courtesy of Rubbermaid®.)

To do list

- ☐ Choose appropriate storage containers.
- ☐ Label storage containers completely.
- ☐ Store holiday decorations safely.
- ☐ Choose an appropriate storage location.

Dealing with Holiday Decorations

Another seasonal storage challenge is storing holiday decorations, especially Christmas items. What often happens is that once the winter holiday season is over, or any holiday for that matter, and you have procrastinated beyond the point of embarrassment, decorations are hastily taken down and literally thrown unsorted into cardboard boxes. If you're lucky, someone might have taken the time to label these boxes—and then again, maybe not. The boxes are put in the garage wherever there is room, and slowly but surely they become buried under a mountain of clutter. Then, when next year rolls around, no one can remember what the boxes looked like, how many there were, or where they might be. As a quick solution, you buy even more to add to the collection you already have!

As with anything you organize, it is important to store like things together, and holiday decorations are no exception. You will want to store decorations for each holiday in their own container. Even if you have a very small quantity of decorations for certain holidays, I would suggest using a smaller container and storing them separately, because this will make accessing them much easier. As a general rule, I would not advocate mixing different holiday decorations within the same container, unless you have such a small quantity that the decorations for each holiday can be easily separated and distinguished by using smaller containers or resealable plastic storage bags within the larger one.

Choosing the appropriate containers will make all the difference in the world in the storage of holiday decorations. All kinds of plastic and cardboard containers can be utilized for this purpose and are available at discount retail stores everywhere. In addition to large see-through containers, which are suitable for any holiday as long as they are properly labeled, there are red and green plastic or cardboard containers in all shapes and sizes for Christmas, blue ones for Hanukkah, bright orange containers with black lids for Halloween, purple containers for Easter, and red ones for the 4th of July. The reason I recommend using colored containers is that you immediately know at a glance which holiday decorations are stored inside without having to read the label.

However, whether you use colored or see-through containers, labeling is still very important. Not only should you label the container with the name of the holiday, but if you have more than one container for each holiday, be sure to specify what is contained within each one. That way, if you decide not to put up all your decorations in any given year, you can find exactly what you are looking for without having to drag everything out. For more information on labeling, see Chapter 2.

Where you store your holiday decorations is almost as important as how you store them. Some people store their holiday decorations up in the attic or other places that are difficult to access. As a result, they often choose not to decorate for a particular holiday because it's inconvenient and too much of a hassle to retrieve the decorations. Although you definitely want to store seasonal decorations on an upper shelf out of the way or in a loft, you don't want them to be so hard to get to that you won't bother to use and enjoy them. Otherwise, what is the point of having them, right?

Things You'll Need

- ❑ Storage containers or boxes
- ❑ Specialized containers for Christmas decorations
- ❑ Self-stick labels or label maker
- ❑ Markers

Storing Christmas Ornaments

Many options are available for storing your Christmas ornaments. Whether you choose to buy a container especially made for this purpose, as shown in Figure 11.2, or use what you have, storage for these items does not have to be an expensive proposition. Regardless of the storage method you choose, it is wise to carefully wrap and protect fragile ornaments to prevent breakage.

As your family opens their holiday presents, be sure to save the used tissue and bubble wrap, which are ideal to wrap ornaments before putting them away.

caution Do not use newspaper to wrap holiday ornaments because the newsprint has a tendency to rub off on the ornaments and can be very difficult and sometimes impossible to remove.

Liquor boxes and other boxes with separated compartments work well for ornament storage. If some of the ornaments are heavier and less fragile than others, be sure to store them on the bottom. In many cases, I do not recommend keeping the original container the ornament came in because this tends to take up too much room. Old food storage containers and holiday cookie tins can be used to store groups of wrapped fragile ornaments, which will protect them well inside a larger box. If you have a lot of small ornaments, egg cartons make excellent storage containers. By the way, this is a great way to store painted Easter eggs, too!

Several types of containers are available that have been especially designed for ornament storage. The unique 14" square storage cube shown in Figure 11.3 features three stackable drawers and holds up to 48 ornaments. Its compact size makes it an easy fit if you are short on storage space.

FIGURE 11.2

This heavy-duty stackable holiday ornament storage container holds up to 52 ornaments. You can't lose the wing lid because it is attached. (Photo courtesy of Organize-Everything.com.)

FIGURE 11.3

This three-tier, see-through storage box for ornaments comes with corrugated dividers and can also be used for crafts and hobbies. (Photo courtesy of Container Store.)

The Holiday Rolling Storage cart shown in Figure 11.4 is one of my all-time favorite organizing products. The six-drawer unit holds up to 72 ornaments and includes drawer dividers. The larger drawers of the three-drawer unit can hold larger items, such as light strands and garlands. Each drawer is easy to access and can be individually labeled. These carts are available at retail stores as well as numerous online retailers, including www.stacksandstacks.com.

FIGURE 11.4
Retrieving and storing holiday ornaments and decorations couldn't be easier than using these heavy-duty rolling carts with drawers. (Photo courtesy of Taylor Gifts.)

DONATING CHRISTMAS DECORATIONS

When Christmas is over and you are taking down your ornaments and decorations, designate and label a "donations box" for decorations you no longer want to keep. Instead of donating this box right away, store it with the rest of your decorations and make a note on your calendar to donate it on October 1st. Most thrift stores do not have adequate storage and will appreciate your donation far more in the fall than they will right after the holiday season is over.

Storing Other Christmas Items

Several options are available for the storage of wreaths. The most economical and easiest is to store them in a heavy-duty garbage bag. If you want to be able to see your wreaths, there are clear, fully zippered wreath bags made for this purpose. However, a no-cost alternative is to save the clear zippered bags in which blankets and comforters are sold and use them for this purpose.

Of course, using a wreath bag will not prevent a wreath from being crushed. If this is a specific concern, a number of clear plastic wreath boxes are available that come in various sizes. Another great alternative is the sturdy soft-sided wreath case made by Rubbermaid®, shown in Figure 11.5, which features a clear side panel that makes it easy to see what's inside and interior support straps to hold the wreath in place. It is available at a number of major discount retailers nationwide.

FIGURE 11.5
The handle on this soft-sided wreath bag not only makes it portable, but easy to hang anywhere for convenient storage. (Photo courtesy of Container Store.)

Lights and garlands can be challenging to store because they can easily get tangled up and damaged. Consider wrapping them around empty cardboard paper towel and gift wrap tubes to avoid this problem. Large five-gallon plastic buckets and popcorn tins can be used to store these items as well. The storage box shown in Figure 11.6 is especially made to store lights and avoid their becoming knotted and twisted. Each box comes with three cord wraps that fit neatly onto rails inside the box, with each one being able to accommodate up to 100 feet of lights or garland.

caution Do not store holiday candles with your decorations because they are likely to warp or melt in the extreme heat.

Artificial Christmas trees can be difficult to store because they are large and bulky, especially if you have limited storage space. The artificial tree storage bag shown in Figure 11.7 is an ideal solution, because it not only stores trees compactly, but also protects them from damage and keeps them clean.

FIGURE 11.6
These easy-stacking polypropylene boxes are an ideal way to store lights and garland tangle-free. (Photo courtesy of Organize-Everything.com.)

FIGURE 11.7
This heavy-duty and water-resistant bag will store artificial trees up to 10' tall. (Photo courtesy of Container Store.)

Summary

I am sure that you have a great sense of accomplishment now that you have completed the organizing portion of this project. You have created logical storage centers for specific types of items, and finding things is going to be so much easier. Undoubtedly, you have installed some wall-mount racks, hooks, or shelving, and you might have even purchased one of the complete storage systems featured in Chapter 4, "Selecting Storage Systems," and throughout the book.

Your garage is really looking great, and now you have to figure out how you are going to get rid of all the stuff you have purged. In Part III, "Beyond the Basics," you will learn the options for enhancing the look of your garage floor, as well as the variety of choices you have for giving, donating, and selling the stuff you no longer need or want.

Part III

Beyond the Basics

Protecting the Garage Floor

12

More than likely, you are reading this chapter for one of these reasons:

- You have finished organizing your entire garage and for the first time in years, you can see the floor. You don't like the way it looks and want to do something about it.

- You bought this book just because this chapter was in it, as you have always longed for a better-looking garage floor.

- You never thought of doing anything to your garage floor until you stumbled on this chapter, but you would consider it.

- You have enjoyed reading this book so much that even though you don't have much interest in doing anything to your garage floor, you thought you would check it out anyway.

I hope your reason is the last one listed, but more than likely, it's the first one. Now that all your stuff is organized and stored properly, those oil stains stand out like a sore thumb, don't they? You have worked hard, organized well, and have bought some new products and, perhaps, an entire new storage system. Things are really looking great—except for the floor. In this chapter, you will learn why people bother to apply coatings or coverings to their garage floor, what one must do in order to prepare the floor, and what kinds of products are available.

Covering the Garage Floor: Should I or Shouldn't I?

How many of you have ever wondered why on earth a person would want to coat their garage floor? After all, it's a garage. What's wrong with a bare concrete floor? You can hose it down, and it requires little or no maintenance. Well, that's true if you don't care how it looks over time and you don't mind living with oil and grease stains, which can be tracked into the house.

Many of you might remember the flaking and blistering gray or green floor coating in garages and basements of yesteryear, and wonder why people ever applied it in the first place. Once they did, they had little choice but to commit to a strict regiment of maintenance and upkeep or strip it all off. So, why bother?

Well, here's why. A concrete floor is porous. If your garage floor is not treated with a sealer or top coating of some kind, it will absorb greasy and oily substances and become easily stained. Obviously, once stains like this begin to form, it is much more difficult to remove them. By thoroughly cleaning your floor and protecting it in some fashion, ongoing maintenance becomes much easier and the floor will look a whole lot better.

The good news is that there are many durable topical coatings and garage floor coverings on the market today that are affordable, will hold up to the abuse, and last much longer than the limited options a few years ago. Some of the newer floor coverings are really good looking and will look fabulous in your newly organized garage. With colors and patterns galore to choose from, you will have no trouble finding something to suit your budget and taste if you decide that you want to go for it.

REMOVING STUBBORN STAINS FROM YOUR GARAGE FLOOR

Oil and grease stains can be tough to remove, but there are many commercially available cleaners and degreasers formulated for this purpose that will remove most of them. Once you have applied the degreaser, scrub the stains with a stiff brush and allow the solution to remain for 15 minutes or more before rinsing. You might have to repeat the process several times to achieve the best results.

Here is one homemade remedy that seems to work fairly well, but it will require some "elbow grease" and repeated applications. Apply dry dishwasher detergent to the stains and let it sit for 45 minutes. Then, pour a small amount of boiling water on the area and scrub vigorously with a stiff brush. Then, rinse thoroughly and repeat the process as necessary.

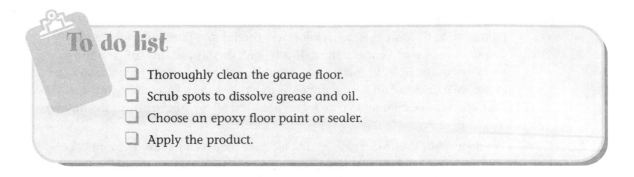

To do list

- ☐ Thoroughly clean the garage floor.
- ☐ Scrub spots to dissolve grease and oil.
- ☐ Choose an epoxy floor paint or sealer.
- ☐ Apply the product.

Using Floor Paints and Sealers

Several kinds of floor paints and sealers are made for covering garage floors. You can apply them yourself or hire a professional. Much of this will depend on your comfort level with doing all the preparation, as well as your budget for this project. This very well could be one of those instances where it is worth paying a professional to do the job for you and save yourself a lot of aggravation. If in doubt, hire the job out!

tip Sprinkle kitty litter or sawdust on grease and oil spots. For better absorption, work it into the stain with your foot, wait a day, and then sweep it up using a broom with stiff bristles.

When painting or sealing a garage floor, you should only use coatings which have been expressly formulated for a garage floor. Otherwise, you will be asking for all kinds of problems—not only in the application of the product, but also its durability. If you don't use coatings that warrant against hot tire peel, you will not be happy with the result; the heat from your tires will actually lift the paint or coating off the floor in no time.

Things You'll Need

- ☐ Floor cleaner/degreaser
- ☐ Rags
- ☐ Broom
- ☐ Stiff brush
- ☐ Garden hose
- ☐ Epoxy product of your choice
- ☐ Clean roller and pads for application

Getting the Floor Ready

If you decide to apply the product yourself, careful and thorough cleaning and preparation of your floor is a must. If you don't do this properly, the coating won't stick—it's that simple. Unfortunately, even the best garage floor paints require an extensive amount of floor preparation before they can be successfully applied. New concrete must be allowed to cure for no less than 30 days before applying any type of coating.

The floor needs to be totally clean, and all spots should be removed. A number of products are available in home improvement stores for this purpose. If the floor has been painted previously, it will need to be stripped, sanded, or scraped to remove all peeling or cracking paint. Even if you think the floor is already clean, be sure to follow the preparation directions printed on the can of the product you have chosen to use.

PREPARING THE FLOOR FOR EPOXY PAINTS

The floor sealer or paint you purchase will provide full details for cleaning and preparing the garage floor, but the process generally involves these steps:

1. Sweep or vacuum the floor thoroughly to remove all loose dirt particles.

2. Wash the entire floor with heavy-duty cleaner and degreaser specifically formulated for this purpose, such as Rust-Oleum's environmentally friendly Industrial Pure Strength 3599™.

3. Use a stiff brush to clean up troublesome oil and grease stains.

4. Rinse the entire floor thoroughly to remove all residue.

5. Etch the floor with commercially available products intended for this purpose. Do not use muriatic acid because it is difficult to neutralize. Rust-Oleum makes an excellent product for this purpose called 108 Cleaning and Etching™ solution. Be sure to follow the product directions.

6. Rinse the entire floor again and allow it to thoroughly dry before applying the epoxy sealer. This will take a minimum of two days and can take longer in areas with high humidity.

7. Vacuum or sweep the floor one more time before applying the epoxy sealer.

Again, be sure to follow the manufacturer's recommendations for preparing the garage floor for the coating you've chosen.

All epoxy product manufacturers will recommend that the floor be etched, using a product specifically formulated for this purpose, before you begin painting; etching roughens the floor surface to provide for better adhesion of the applied paint or stain. Some epoxy products might require you to use a special primer coat as well, so read the directions carefully.

Selecting and Applying an Appropriate Product

Not all epoxy products are created equally, so don't buy one based on price. You can find a number of good high-performance products at your local specialized paint dealer. With any of the do-it-yourself epoxy products featured in this section, be sure to follow the directions on the can exactly. Use a clean roller or pad to apply the product; for most of these products, two coats will be required.

caution

Always wear safety goggles and rubber gloves when using cleaning and etching solutions to prepare your garage floor for epoxy sealers, as well as when applying the sealer itself. Be sure that the area in which you are working is well ventilated.

After the epoxy sealer has been applied, wait the prescribed amount of time recommended by the manufacturer, plus a few days, just to be safe and account for variations in temperature and humidity. Be sure to plan this project when you know you can remain off the garage floor for the recommended period of time and gather up anything you might need beforehand. Remember that the surface can feel dry to the touch but might not be thoroughly cured underneath. It's just not worth the risk of walking or driving on it too soon, is it? Although it is generally safe to walk on your newly coated floor in three days, most manufacturers will recommend waiting seven days before driving on it. Garage guru Bill West recommends waiting 14 days to be sure your floor is fully cured.

Behr has developed the 1-Part Epoxy Acrylic system, which is especially formulated for the garage. It is sold at The Home Depot and is available in 40 custom colors, but it can be color-matched to your walls. American Tradition Epoxy is a two-component system that comes with a five-year warranty. It is sold at Lowe's and is available in 42 tints with a semi-gloss finish. Both products come with a non-skid additive that can be mixed in to provide greater traction. To avoid clumping, Bill West recommends that you broadcast the non-skid additive like sowing seed over the fresh application of epoxy.

EPOXYShield by Rust-Oleum is easy to apply and maintain. The kit includes a concentrated surface cleaner, which eliminates the need for etching and primers, and a video with complete installation instructions. The water-based two-part epoxy system is available in two colors at Lowe's for less than $60 per kit. Each kit will cover approximately 250 square feet of smooth, bare concrete (about the size of a one-car garage), and rough, porous concrete may require more. For additional information, visit www.rustoleum.com.

PremierGarage®, a fast-growing network of garage-enhancement specialists, offers a groundbreaking and innovative urethane floor coating, shown in Figure 12.1, that is professionally applied by one of its 50 franchisees nationwide. This one-of-a-kind technology allows for a durable floor coating to be installed in just one day, and you can drive on it the next. (Yes, you read that right!) Oil stains are easily wiped up from this slick finish, which comes in six solid colors called PremierOne™ or five granite styles called PremierOnePlus™. The floor boasts superior UV, chemical, and abrasion resistance with a long-lasting shine in addition to a limited warranty against peeling and staining as well as defects in materials or workmanship. PremierGarage® also manufactures and installs a full line of wall-mount garage storage cabinets and Schulte® activity organizer products. For more information and to find a location near you, visit www.premiergarage.com.

FIGURE 12.1
You can install this revolutionary, tough, easy-to-maintain floor today and drive on it tomorrow! (Photo courtesy of PremierGarage®.)

Investing in a Floor Covering

Depending on the size of your garage floor and your budget, you might want to consider investing in a floor covering instead of applying an epoxy sealer. This not only will save you some time and effort, but you might be pleasantly surprised at the little difference in price, especially if you had thought about hiring a professional to do the job. Many of the floor coverings offered today are so easy to install that you can do the job yourself. They are also easy to maintain.

One of the more recent entrants into the polypropylene flooring market is the durable and easy-to-clean interlocking Fast-Flor tile system by Acclaim Designs and Profiles, Inc., located in Canada. Not only are these snap-together tiles, shown in Figure 12.2, easy to install, they can be laid right on top of stained and uneven surfaces with no preparation. These one-foot-square tiles are available in seven colors to create any number of designs. For more information, visit www.homeorganizers.ca.

No glue or tools are required to lay these anti-slip interlocking tiles that resist mold, mildew, and most chemicals. See the difference for yourself. (Photo courtesy of Fast-Flor.)

The poly-vinyl Parking Pad®, shown in Figure 12.3, resists most stains and is built to last. The ribbed construction traps debris and water and provides a non-skid walking surface. Garage guru Bill West, author of *Your Garagenous Zone*, has driven on his Parking Pad® with four studded snow tires and claims that it shows no sign of punctures! The pads come in six standard sizes and colors, ranging in price from $150 to $250, and can be used to cover the entire garage floor. The Parking Pad® is available at numerous online retailers as well as Lowe's and Menard's stores nationwide. It can also be professionally installed by many GarageTek® and The Accessory Group dealers. For additional information or to locate a distributor in your area, visit the Better Life Technology website at www.bltllc.com.

The G-Floor®, shown in Figure 12.4, is an even heavier-duty version of the Parking Pad® and can be used indoors in basements, utility rooms, and laundry rooms. It comes in a satin finish ribbed or coin pattern, which can be shined with Shinekeeper® by Armstrong® to give it a glossy sheen, if you prefer, and to provide even more protection. It is available in three standard sizes and at slightly less than twice the price of the Parking Pad®.

FIGURE 12.3
Installation is so easy. Just roll out the Parking Pad® and cut it to fit. No glue is required. (Photo courtesy of Better Life Technology.)

FIGURE 12.4
This heavy-duty G-Floor® coin pattern comes in six colors and is easy to keep clean with a hose or a broom. (Photo courtesy of Better Life Technology.)

Summary

I'll bet you weren't even aware that so many options existed for enhancing the look of your garage floor, were you? You probably thought you were destined to live with that stained and drab-looking concrete floor forever, unless you wanted to spend a lot of money to do something about it. At least now you know that there are lots of affordable choices, and you just need to make up your mind as to which one is right for you and fits your budget.

Whether you decide to seal, paint, buy a floor covering, or leave the concrete bare, the choice is yours. I am sure that some of you can't be bothered, whereas others of you are now inspired to go for it. The good thing is that you don't have to do anything right away—or you could just go ahead and treat yourself as your reward for doing such a great job of organizing. Why not? You deserve it!

In the meantime, you still need to get rid of all the items you've culled during your garage organization. As you move to the next chapter, you will learn about the many options you have for donating, selling, tossing, or recycling all the things you have purged throughout your garage-organizing experience. Who knows? You might just make enough money by selling your discarded treasures on eBay or in a garage sale, or with the tax savings you reap from your donations, to pay for that new garage floor!

Getting Rid of Stuff

13

Congratulations on a job well done! With your garage neatly organized, you are probably wondering what you are going to do with all the stuff you no longer want. Whether you have devoted a couple hours or several days to your garage-organizing project, you have undoubtedly accumulated lots of things you need to get rid of, ranging from discarded clothing and household and seasonal items, to tools, lawn and garden equipment, and sports gear. More than likely, you also have some hazardous and toxic waste that will require safe disposal.

You have many ways to accomplish the task ahead, ranging from throwing things away to turning your discarded treasures into cash. This chapter will focus on tossing and recycling options, properly disposing of hazardous and toxic waste, giving things away, and selling items of value. Your ultimate decision will depend on how much time you have and how fast you would like the items to disappear. No matter which method you choose, the most important consideration is to dispose of things in an environmentally friendly and responsible way.

To do list

- ☐ Bag up your trash.
- ☐ Put your trash at the curb or take it to the dump.
- ☐ Arrange to have someone pick up your trash (if applicable).

Tossing and Recycling Options

One of the simplest and fastest methods for disposing of items you no longer want is by tossing or recycling them. Obviously, things that are broken, not recyclable, and would be of no value to anyone else should be tossed. If you have a large volume of stuff to discard, use heavy-duty trash bags and funnel them out with your weekly garbage over a period of weeks. Make sure you know the maximum limit your local trash pickup service will accept.

Things You'll Need

- ☐ Trash can
- ☐ Heavy-duty trash bags
- ☐ Rope (if applicable)

Some municipalities have regularly scheduled bulk trash pickup days or will allow you to schedule one yourself free of charge. On a bulk pickup day, there is usually no limit to the size or quantity of the items you are allowed to place at the curb. Check with your city or private trash company to learn what services it offers. If you don't want to have all that trash sitting around while waiting for the next bulk trash pickup day, another option is to find the name of a local trash hauler in the newspaper or in the Yellow

caution

When taking things to the city dump yourself, be sure that you have secured the load safely with rope so that items do not fall off onto the roadway while you are en route. Not only is this littering, but it makes the road unsafe for other drivers.

Pages who will come and take it all away for a fee. Alternatively, if you have a truck, you can take the trash to the dump yourself, as shown in Figure 13.1.

FIGURE 13.1

Tie down your junk and don't be guilty of littering up the roadway. (Photo courtesy of Center for Organization.)

One of the newest and fastest-growing franchise businesses today is 1-800-GOT-JUNK?® With more than 100 locations in North America, these people come to your home or office in their 10-foot-long trucks, as shown in Figure 13.2, and load up all your junk, which is then recycled or taken to the landfill. Their drivers can haul away anything that two people can lift, except for hazardous and toxic waste. They will even climb up into your attic and lift the heaviest and bulkiest of items at no extra charge and take discarded mattresses and broken appliances that no one else will.

Scheduling a pickup is easily arranged by calling the 1-800-GOT-JUNK?® toll-free number or visiting their website at www.1800gotjunk.com. Pricing is based on your location, as well as the volume and type of material being hauled away, and includes all labor, landfill, and weight charges. You can get a ballpark price on the phone and an exact price will be quoted onsite. In most cases, the cost will be lower than the price of having a dumpster delivered.

To do list

- [ ] Determine whether you have any hazardous waste.
- [ ] Learn disposal options in your area.
- [ ] Take hazardous and toxic waste to the proper site or arrange for it to be picked up.

FIGURE 13.2
Fully licensed and insured drivers will call you 30 minutes before arrival to let you know they are on their way. (Photo courtesy of 1-800-GOT-JUNK?®)

Dealing with Hazardous Waste and Toxic Substances

It is important for everyone to share in the responsibility of protecting our environment and disposing of hazardous and toxic wastes properly. If these types of products are thrown into the trash, along with everything else, this can have long-term effects on our surroundings and affect humans, animals, and plants. If hazardous waste is dumped in a landfill, it can emit harmful vapors and seep into our drinking water supplies, as well as rivers, lakes, and oceans.

Federal, state, and local laws require hazardous and toxic substances to be disposed of in accordance with prescribed regulations. It is your responsibility to determine whether something is classified as hazardous waste. If you are caught disposing of these items improperly, you can be fined and imprisoned in some cases. It is imperative that you check with local and state agencies to learn the procedures for safe disposal of such items in your area.

Determining Whether a Substance Is Toxic or Hazardous

Most hazardous substances include precautionary statements and disposal instructions on the front or back label and will include the words *poison*, *danger*, *flammable*, *warning*, or *toxic*. If the substance is a corrosive acid or reactive when mixed with other chemicals, it falls into this category. If it is a substance that you know would be unsafe to drink and harmful to your health, it would be considered hazardous waste. If you are unsure about whether a product falls into this category, call the place where it is sold and they will usually know.

So what kinds of products are toxic? More than you could ever imagine. Look under your sinks, in the kitchen, bathroom, utility room, garage, and your shed if you have one. These products are everywhere. Table 13.1 shows a partial list of the many substances found around the home that would be considered hazardous waste.

Table 13.1   How Many of These Hazardous and Toxic Substances Do You Have Around Your House?

Acids	Hair and nail products
Aerosols	Insecticides
Asbestos	Medicines
Auto products (antifreeze, brake and transmission fluids, tire cleaners, motor oil)	Lawn-care products (fertilizers, herbicides, pesticides, weed-killer products)
Batteries	Mercury (fluorescent bulbs, thermometers, thermostats)
Cleaners (oven, drain, toilet bowl)	Mothballs
Cooking oil	Paint and paint thinners
Degreasers	Photographic chemicals
Dyes	Polishes
Empty tanks (helium, gas, propane	Pool chemicals
Fertilizers	Preservatives
Fuels	Solvents and strippers
Glues (rubber cement)	Spot, stain, and rust removers

Disposing of Hazardous Wastes and Toxic Substances

So what do you do with all the hazardous chemicals and substances that no one wants and you are not permitted to throw in the garbage? Most municipalities have a hazardous waste disposal hotline number you can call and ask where to dispose of particular substances. This number can usually be found in the government listings section of the Yellow Pages. Once you know the location, simply drive there and drop the substances off, usually at no charge. If you would like someone to come and pick the substances up, look in the Yellow Pages under *Hazardous Materials Disposal*. Of course, there will be a charge for this service.

An Arizona-based company called Earth 911 (www.earth911.org/master.asp or www.cleanup.org) is a national environmental network where you can enter your zip code to locate the recycling or hazardous waste collection center nearest you. Their information comes from thousands of sources and makes searching easy. If you don't have web access, they can be reached by calling 1-800-CLEANUP.

Giving Things Away

One of the easiest ways to get rid of stuff is by giving it away. There are all kinds of people and organizations that desperately need what you no longer want and just can't afford to buy it themselves. You can give directly to individuals or donate to any number of organizations that will make sure what you donate gets into the hands of those who need it most.

Giving to Individuals

I am sure you have often heard the expression that one person's trash is another person's treasure. One surprisingly easy way to give things away is by putting them at the curb with a sign that says "FREE" on it. You will be amazed at how fast those old computer desks, bookshelves, and lawn tools will disappear. However, if items sit there for more than two days, then probably no one does want them and you should bring the stuff back in so your neighbors don't get upset with you.

FIND A NEW HOME FOR YOUR STUFF ON FREECYCLE

Did you ever wish that there was a listing somewhere of stuff people wanted to give away for free and you could just put your old mattress on it and wait for the phone to ring? Well, now there is. It's on the Internet with almost 2,000 cities participating around the world. It's called Freecycle and functions like a free eBay. Simply list what you no longer need or want on a message board and people will offer to take it off your hands. The only rule is that no money is exchanged and that the item is legal and appropriate for all ages. You can give it to the first person who responds or to the individual you believe to be the neediest... it's up to you.

Freecycle also works in reverse. If you need something, post your request on the message board, and others can answer your posting if they want to give what you are asking for. You will be amazed at the things that appear on the message board that are being given away... free! For more information or to try it yourself, visit www.freecycle.org.

Donating to Organizations

Many people like to donate to their favorite organizations and charities and get a tax write-off while doing something good. The list of great causes is endless, and some of them will even come to your house and pick the stuff up. All you need to do is choose the charity, and the rest is easy. Look in the Yellow Pages under *Charities*, *Social Service*, or *Welfare Organizations*. Many cities and towns will have a number of organizations that are unique to that area. Table 13.2 lists some national organizations that are always looking for donations of items to give away or sell in their thrift stores.

> **tip**
> If you are having difficulty in finding a charity that is right for you, consider donating to local high school theater groups or vocational classes. If the items are in good condition, your church or synagogue might want them for the annual rummage sale.

Table 13.2   National Charities Where You Can Donate

Name of Charity	Website for More Information
The Arc	www.thearc.org
Bethesda	www.blhs.org
Goodwill Industries	www.goodwill.org
Habitat for Humanity	www.habitat.org
The Salvation Army	www.salvationarmyusa.org
Society of St. Vincent de Paul	www.svdpusa.org

Often, you want to find just the right charity for a specific type of item you want to donate. Table 13.3 lists some types of items and places where you can either drop off the items or find more information on donating or recycling them.

Table 13.3   Places to Donate Specific Items

Items to Be Donated or Recycled	Store Drop-off Sites/ Websites for More Information
Batteries	Lowe's, www.rbrc.org, www.batteryrecycling.com
Bicycles	www.ibike.org/encouragement/freebike.htm
Blankets and towels	Your local animal shelter, www.pets911.com
Books	Local libraries, charities, hospitals
Cell phones	Verizon and Sprint stores, Franklin Covey stores, Office Depot, www.wirelessfoundation.org
Clothing	www.DressForSuccess.org, www.GlassSlipperProject.org

Table 13.3   Continued

Items to Be Donated or Recycled	Store Drop-off Sites/ Websites for More Information
Computers	Goodwill Industries, www.dell.com, www.cristina.org
Eyeglasses	Lions Clubs, www.lenscrafters.com
Hangers	Any dry cleaners
Motor oil	Jiffy Lube
Paint	Habitat for Humanity
Steel	www.recycle-steel.org

DON'T FORGET YOUR BEST FRIENDS!

Americans are known for their love of animals, especially their four-legged furry friends. And with that love comes all the pet paraphernalia that goes along with it. But what happens when our pets outgrow their collar or harness or bed, lose interest in their toys, or pass away? If you're like many, this stuff just sits in the garage taking up space. But think of all those worthy animals at your local animal shelter who desperately await homes and could benefit from these items you (and your pet) no longer need. Animal shelters operate on tight budgets and would be happy to have your old pet dishes and toys, crates, leashes, blankets, towels, and pet-grooming aids. If you're in doubt about whether an item could be useful to a local animal shelter, just call and ask! You might be surprised at the uses these resourceful and needy organizations can find for your unwanted but still functioning furnishings, child gates, shovels, pans, containers, and more. You can find local shelters in your Yellow Pages or by visiting www.pets911.com and clicking the Find a Local Shelter button to locate several in your geographic area. What a great way to teach your children the importance of giving and treating animals humanely.

Giving for All Its Worth

When donating items to charities and other nonprofit organizations, you are entitled to deduct these donations on your taxes if you itemize your deductions. The IRS allows you to calculate the fair market value of the donated items or the amount someone would be willing to pay if you sold them. However, most people tend to guesstimate and undervalue what their stuff is worth and do not take the maximum deduction allowed. One way to get help in calculating the fair market value of items you donate is by reading IRS Publication 561, "Determining the Value of Donated Property," which is available at www.irs.gov.

Another way to determine the fair market value of items you donate is by using TurboTax® ItsDeductible® software by Intuit, shown in Figure 13.3. You simply enter the donated items, and the software will provide the accurate fair market value based on the item quality in compliance with IRS guidelines. ItsDeductible® takes all the guesswork out of the process and will help you achieve the full, legal deduction allowed by the IRS. If your deduction is over $500, the software will automatically fill out Form 8283, which is required by the IRS to be submitted with your tax return. The program can be purchased online and downloaded at www.itsdeductible.com for $19.95.

FIGURE 13.3
Don't guess what your tax-deductible donations are worth. Let TurboTax® ItsDeductible® software calculate it for you. (Photo courtesy of Intuit.)

Selling Items for Profit

If you are determined to sell what you can and turn your trash into cash, there are a number of ways this can be accomplished. The amount you can make is only limited by how industrious you are and how much time you are willing to devote to the process.

One of the oldest ways to sell items is by listing them for sale in the local newspaper. Prices will vary, and some newspapers will let you place ads to sell items valued at less than $50 for free. When you sell items through a newspaper, you will need to list your telephone number and screen the calls yourself, which can be a drawback and safety consideration for some.

A more modern way to achieve the same result is to list your items for sale on eBay. If your items are smaller and can be easily mailed, you can list them on the national eBay registry. If the items are large and cost-prohibitive to ship, you can use local eBay listings for your area. On an eBay auction, your items will bring the highest price that someone is willing to pay for the specified time of the auction, but you can set a reserve price to make sure that the item doesn't sell for less than it's worth.

EBAY THE EASY WAY

If you don't know how to sell on eBay and don't want to learn, many eBay specialists have sprung up all over the country who will take care of everything for you—from taking the photos and listing the item, to collecting the payment and shipping the item to the highest bidder—for a portion of the proceeds. You don't need to do anything except drop off the item at their location. If you keep saying that you want to sell something on eBay, but never seem to get around to it, this could be the solution you have been waiting for. For more information, visit www.baylisters.com or www.auctiondrop.com.

Another service similar to Freecycle is Craig's List (www.craigslist.org). The only difference is that on Craig's List, money is allowed to change hands, so all sorts of things can be bought and sold. In addition to buying and selling items, you can rent an apartment, search for a job, and find a new car or a potential mate—all with no advertising and banner ads to wade through. The only fee currently being charged is for job postings in New York, Los Angeles, and San Francisco.

> **tip** Consider partnering with a consignment store if you have just a few large items of furniture to sell. If they are interested in what you have, many stores will offer to pick up your items. Consignment stores charge varying rates of commission and their policies vary from store to store, but expect to split the proceeds equally with them.

If you are the entrepreneurial sort and have a large quantity of items you would like to sell, why not host your own garage sale? You might want to try that first and utilize some of the methods mentioned in this chapter for the items you have left. For more information to help you decide if it is worth your time and effort, as well as all the guidance you need to have a successful one, be sure to read Chapter 14, "Having a Successful Garage Sale."

Summary

There is no right or wrong way to get rid of the stuff you have purged during the process of organizing your garage. You just need to decide how much time you have and whether it is more important to make some money or to take the tax deduction.

For some, the money will come in real handy to buy some of the organizing products, garage storage systems, or floor coverings you have read about in this book. For others, you just want to get rid of this stuff as fast as possible; otherwise, you might be tempted to change your mind and not let it go.

Regardless of the choice you make, pat yourself on the back for the awesome job you have done. Don't break that promise to yourself to keep things organized from now on. Remember, unless you make the commitment to maintain your new organizational system, you could slip back into old habits very quickly. But, I am confident that you have worked much too hard on this project to let that happen.

So, enjoy your new, uncluttered garage every time you drive in and be good to yourself—you deserve it!

Having a Successful Garage Sale

I must confess... I love a good garage sale. Perhaps it's my entrepreneurial wheeler-dealer spirit that makes it so much fun for me to host one and watch things I no longer want turn into money. Or maybe it is my insatiable quest for a good bargain that makes it so hard for me to resist the impulse to pull over and stop at one. Whatever the case, I'm hooked on the fun I have and enjoy the challenge.

All successful garage sales share two characteristics: The shoppers find great bargains, and the seller takes in enough money to compensate for the effort and time spent getting ready for the sale. The best way to ensure that your sale will be included in this category is having realistic expectations and undergoing thorough planning and preparation.

In reading the previous chapter about choosing places to donate or get rid of the things you don't want, you very well might have found yourself saying, "I paid too much for this to give it away" or "Someone would pay a lot of money to have this." In fact, you could be totally correct that someone would pay a considerable sum to relieve you of some of your items. However, if you have only a few items of any real value, you need to determine whether it is worth your time and trouble to have a sale.

To do list

- ☐ Check local ordinances to determine whether garage sales are allowed in your neighborhood.
- ☐ Assess the value of the items you want to sell and whether you have enough items to make a garage sale worthwhile.
- ☐ Determine whether you have time to prepare and conduct a sale, how accessible your site will be for the general public, and how much help you'll need in conducting the sale.

Deciding Whether a Garage Sale Is Worth It

You have many items to consider before rushing into a decision to have a garage sale. Yes, you will undoubtedly make some money, and many of you would rather have the cash than the tax-saving benefits of making a donation. On the flip side, once you figure out the amount of time and preparation having a garage sale is going to take, it could end up being a losing proposition all the way around.

Ask yourself the following questions as you decide whether a sale will be worthwhile:

- Does your city, town, or housing community allow garage sales? Some cities and towns expressly prohibit people from having garage sales, and others require you to obtain an inexpensive permit to do so. Check with the local authorities and find out if there are any restrictions or legal requirements in your area. The last thing you want to do is go through all this preparation and be fined or have your sale closed down. And while you are at it, be sure to inquire if there are any rules about putting signs up in your neighborhood to advertise it.

- How many "big-ticket" items do you have to sell? If you have several large pieces of furniture that you need to get rid of, having a garage sale can be one of the simplest ways to move this stuff out. If you don't have any big-ticket items, consider how many 10-cent plastic food storage containers and $1 T-shirts you will need to sell to make enough to go out to dinner at a good restaurant or buy a nice outfit. If you are expecting to make enough to cover your next mortgage payment, don't count on it.

- Do you have the necessary time it will take to prepare for the sale? To have a successful garage sale, you will need to devote several days and evenings to gathering the merchandise, sorting and pricing it, placing ads, making signs, and setting up the sale. If you barely have time to go to the grocery or take your clothes to the dry cleaner, how are you going to carve out the time to have a garage sale?

- Will you be able to generate enough traffic? If you live in a place that is off the beaten path and difficult to find with very limited parking, even the best signs in the world might not direct enough people there, and you are setting yourself up for failure.

- Will you have people to help on the day of the sale? To have a garage sale of any size, you are going to need assistance on the day of the sale, especially in the first three hours. Depending on the size of the sale, you might need help even longer. Not only will shoppers have questions, but the more helpers you have to interact with shoppers, the better your bottom line will be. Unless you have very few items to sell, don't attempt to undertake this on your own.

One of the best ways to determine whether a garage sale is going to be worth the time and effort you spend preparing for it is to make a list of the major items you want to sell. List the price you think you could get—not necessarily the price you would like, but what you think someone would pay—and be realistic. People are looking for bargains. In other words, what would you pay if you were hunting for this same item in a garage sale? Now, add up the 10 highest priced items and ask yourself if allocating virtually all your spare time the week prior to the sale and getting up early and devoting the entire weekend of the sale is worth that amount. If it is, go for it, and continue reading this chapter for all the guidance you need to have a successful garage sale. If you have decided that it isn't worth your time for the limited return, go back to Chapter 13, "Getting Rid of Stuff," and choose an alternative for getting rid of the stuff you don't want.

To do list

- ❑ Schedule the sale.
- ❑ Gather and price the merchandise.
- ❑ Advertise the sale.
- ❑ Set up the sale.

Preparing for the Big Day

Having a successful garage sale is a lot of work, and every moment you spend planning will be well worth it in the long run and help ensure that the event is profitable. You cannot begin too early, because the last thing you want to do is stay up the entire night before, pricing items and making signs. You need to be well rested so you will be at your best on the day of the sale as you interact with the public; you want to be the best salesperson you can be.

Use the information in Table 14.1 to guide you in creating a timeline as you prepare for the big day. Remember that these are just estimates; some of you will need more or less time, depending on your individual circumstances.

Table 14.1　Timetable for Planning a Garage Sale

Timeframe	Tasks
One month before	Choose a date and designate the large items you want to sell. Save paper and plastic bags from the grocery store for items purchased.
Three weeks before	Go through the house and make a clean sweep through each room. Box up the things you would like to sell. Ask each family member to do the same.
Two weeks before	Place an ad in newspapers with early deadlines. Gather up stuff from the house and garage and begin sorting. Group like things together—books with books, toys with toys, and so on. This will help you price and merchandise the sale.
One week before	Place an ad in the daily newspaper.
Three to five days before	Price the items.
Two days before	Make signs. Go to the bank and get your cashbox ready.
Day before	Go through the house one more time to gather more items and set up the sale.
Morning of sale	Place signs in strategic locations.

Things You'll Need

- ❏ Pen and paper
- ❏ Calendar
- ❏ Price tags
- ❏ Poster board
- ❏ Marking pens
- ❏ Tables for merchandise

Choosing a Date and a Time

It is important to choose your date wisely—this detail alone will significantly affect whether you will generate the necessary traffic to reel in the big bucks. The time of year is important, and the month you choose will greatly depend on where you live. If you live in the northern, colder climates, May through October are usually the best months. How many garage sales would you expect to see in December and January in Minnesota? In the southern climates of Florida, Texas, and Arizona, you will want to avoid the intense heat of the summer and focus on spring, fall, and winter. December is a hit-or-miss month because many people are shopping at the malls and not cruising for used bargain items. No matter where you live, be sure to avoid the typically rainy months in your area.

Consider talking with your neighbors and try to make this a neighborhood or multi-family event. Shoppers love being able to attend several sales in the same neighborhood—the more the merrier! Not only will this increase the traffic, but everyone can share in the time and expense of placing the ads and making the signs.

Saturday is definitely the most popular day of the weekend for a garage sale, but it has become a common trend to begin a sale on Friday. Professional garage sale shoppers like to get a jump start on everyone else and see what you have. They will also help spread the word if you have things they know other people might want. Although your actual traffic might not be as high on Friday, your sales could easily be better than what you will make on Saturday and Sunday.

By holding a sale on Saturday, you have the option of opening for business on Sunday if you didn't sell everything you wanted to. Extending the sale into Sunday also gives people a chance to come back with their trucks and pick up larger items they were not able to take with them on Friday or Saturday. If you live near a church, do not overlook Sunday as a great opportunity to catch the after-church crowd.

Holiday weekends can be a good time to schedule a sale, but stick to the Saturday and Sunday schedule because Monday's don't seem to attract as many shoppers. If you live near a college campus, Labor Day is an excellent weekend to have a garage sale because college students need to outfit their apartments.

tip If you can schedule your sale to coincide with a church rummage sale, this will increase your traffic. Also, remember, many people get paid on the 1st and 15th day of the month, so sales closely following these dates are more likely to generate a paying crowd.

caution Although you have done everything possible to schedule your sale at the best possible time, no one can predict when it will rain. If you are having a one-day sale, plan for the next day to be the rain date and advertise it as such.

Whether you want to or not, plan on beginning your sale at 8 a.m. or even earlier. I know that it's your sale and you might not be an early bird, but this is one time when it will be well worth the effort to get up and open those doors early. Serious garage sale hunters start early and are finished by noon. They plan their route, and if all the other sales open at 8 a.m., do you think they are going to backtrack because you didn't want to start your sale until 10 a.m.? Even if you advertise your sale to start at 8 a.m., shoppers will begin lining up as early as 7 a.m. to be sure they don't miss out on a bargain. You will have the most activity and make most of your money in the first few hours of your sale, and you will be cutting into your profits if you don't open early.

There really isn't much point in printing a closing time. People expect you to stay open until noon, and if business is good, you can stay open as long as you like. Some of my best sales have happened in the middle of the afternoon. Besides, if you are going to donate whatever remains, you can always putter out in the garage or schedule some outdoor chores, which will let you assist anyone who happens to stop by. When it slows down and you are tired, take down your signs and close your garage door.

Determining a Selling Price

The first rule of thumb is to price reasonably; otherwise, you will defeat your whole purpose for doing this. Remember, you are having a garage sale—not opening a department store—and people are looking for bargains. Your ultimate goal is to get rid of this stuff and to make as much money as you can while you're at it. The less stuff you have left at the end of the sale means that it was successful. I know that you don't want to give your stuff away, but it's not going to do anyone much good if you are left with just about everything because you wouldn't come down on your price. This is not a time to be proud or greedy. It's a time to wheel and deal, have some fun, and get rid of your stuff!

One school of thought on pricing is that you can always start out high and come down if someone is interested. However, this strategy can backfire, because if people feel that everything is priced too high, they will leave frustrated and not even bother to ask you if you will take less.

There are numerous pricing formulas to make sure that you don't overprice and find yourself stuck with lots of things that don't sell. Unless they are antiques or have an obvious value, most of your ordinary household items will bring only a fraction of their original cost. A good rule of thumb for most things is to start with the price you paid or determine what the cost of the item would be if it were new and then price it at somewhere between 10 to 30 percent of its original price. This formula will vary with the individual item, and its condition and does not apply to antiques! Clothing will most definitely fall at the lower end of the range—and even lower unless it's vintage or in perfect condition—and household appliances will sell closer to the top of the range. If you want $5 for an item and won't take less, price it at $6, so you will have room to bargain and negotiate with potential buyers.

If you have antiques or vintage items for sale, check eBay to get a reasonable estimate of their value. With this figure in mind, you can determine how much you are willing to let an item go for in the sale, and if it doesn't sell there, you can sell it on eBay afterward. Even if you can get more for something on eBay, don't forget to take shipping costs into account.

tip Over the years, I have learned the following lesson time and time again.
People are often looking for specific things. Yes, they are looking for bargains of all kinds, but they know what they want. When a person expresses interest in an item, be ready and willing to deal with them right then and there. Assume that this is the only person who is going to express interest in it and want to buy it all day, because this could very well be the case. Isn't it worth taking a little less for an item than you had hoped for rather than be stuck with it at the end of the day?

Most people already know that half the fun of buying at a garage sale is bargaining, and rarely does one pay the price that an item is marked. It still doesn't hurt to have a large visible "Make Offer" sign just to remind and encourage them to make offers.

TAGGING YOUR TREASURES

A golden rule for a successful garage sale is to have everything priced with a tag. The last thing you want is for people needing to ask the price of every single item and you having to quickly come up with a price on the spot. It wastes everyone's time and is a certain recipe to ensure that you won't sell many items or make as much you could. Even the smallest of items should have a price tag, so people don't have to ask. And whatever you do, don't save all this pricing for the night before or the morning of the sale. It can be more time consuming than you think.

If you don't want to tag every single item, you can get around this by charging one price for a particular kind of item, such as $1 for vinyl record albums, 50 cents for all T-shirts, or 25 cents for all plastic food storage containers. You can have boxes labeled with "All items for $1 or 50 cents." If you don't want to bother with marking things a dime, have a "Two items for 25 cents" box. The only downside to this is that everyone working the sale needs to understand the system or there can be some confusion at the check out.

All kinds of price tags and self-stick labels are available. It is best to make up a batch of price tags in advance and mark those 25 cents, 50 cents, 75 cents, $1, $1.50, and so on. This will help the pricing process go much faster rather than you having to stop and write one as you price each item.

Be sure that your tags are large enough to write a markdown price. If they aren't, you can place a second tag next to the original price tag to show the reduced price. Consider marking down items once the initial rush of the first few hours has passed. This will just help shoppers feel like they are getting even more of a bargain! As a matter of fact, sometimes after I price an item and immediately decide that the price is too high, I just "X" it out so the old price is still readable and write the lower price next to it rather than make a new tag.

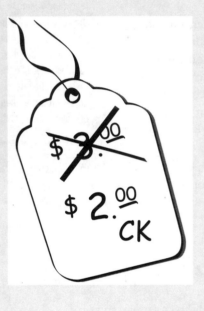

FIGURE 14.1
Bargain hunters like to know when an item has been reduced. The initials enable the cashier to properly credit the sale.

You can buy various colors of price tags to denote different prices or to differentiate items in a multifamily sale. Another way to designate between items in a sale of this type is by writing people's initials next to the price, as shown in Figure 14.1. This way, the cashier will know who gets credit for the sale.

If you don't want to buy price tags and you have an excess of file folder labels, they are an excellent substitute. One sheet of labels can generate a lot of price tags by cutting it into strips. Masking tape is not as good for pricing as self-stick labels because it comes off easily and the writing often smears, but it does work very well on clothing.

Advertising Your Sale

If you are willing to spend some money for marketing, newspaper ads are an excellent vehicle to advertise your sale. Many professional garage sale devotees peruse the paper and devise a route to make sure they don't miss a bargain, and this is the best way to ensure that you will be included on their list. Remember, your goal is to generate as much traffic as you can and for as many people as possible to view your treasures. Not everyone is in the market for the same thing, and some shoppers have a very specific shopping list.

The cost for a newspaper ad is usually quite low because many cities offer a reduced rate for these types of ads and will even throw in a garage sale kit, including some signs. Take advantage of the three- and four-day specials many newspapers offer and be sure to begin advertising your sale on Thursday at the latest, even if it is a one-day-only sale to be held on Saturday. Other ways to promote your sale include the use of the Internet, local bulletin boards, and newsletters of various types.

In addition to stating the dates and time of the sale, be as specific as possible when describing your sale. Include a reasonably detailed description of the items you are selling. Obviously, it is important to include as many of your "big-ticket" items as possible, because just selling these can make the entire enterprise worthwhile and everything else you sell will be gravy. Include any verbiage that applies, such as multifamily sale, 20 years of accumulation, everything must go, antiques, collectibles, vintage clothing, TVs, lots of furniture, like-new washer/dryer, and so on.

> **tip**
>
> Be sure to include your address and directions if necessary, but do not include your telephone number unless you are willing to entertain numerous calls asking about what you will be selling or if the caller can stop by the day before because he or she can't come the day of the sale.

Making and Posting Signs

There is little doubt that good signage is critical to the success of your sale. You might wonder why this would be so important in the days of Internet maps and directional services. First, if you live in a place that is difficult to find, signs will help direct shoppers to you so they don't get lost. Second, there's a whole world of shoppers out there who have no idea about your sale and no intention of going to one until they see your sign. I will call these the "impulse" shoppers, who could turn out to be your best customers because they will make many impulse purchases. I can imagine you might be thinking that this is hypocritical coming from a professional organizer who professes that people should clear their lives and spaces of clutter and not accumulate countless things they don't need. But the fact remains that there will always be impulse buyers, so you might as well attract them to *your* sale and reap the benefit.

A good garage sale sign should be noticeable and easy to read quickly, as the one shown in Figure 14.2. Use bright colors and don't crowd too much information on it. Consider attaching a few helium balloons to your signs to attract more attention. The following information should be included on your sign:

- Kind of sale: Garage, Estate, Multifamily
- Date(s) and time
- Address
- Special items of interest
- Directional arrows

This sign has all the essential information to entice and direct people to the sale.

Antiques **Multi-Family** Furniture
Garage Sale
Saturday Only, June 6
8AM
5065 West Elm
Everything Must Go!

One of my favorite signs is the kind that fits in a frame that sticks in the ground. Your Realtor® might loan you a frame, or you can mount your sign on a wooden stake or a coat hanger. One advantage to signs like these is that they can be viewed from both sides.

You will need to get up extra early and allow some time in the morning to post your signs just before you are ready to open the garage door. It is wise to designate one person whose job it will be to strategically place the signs so prospective shoppers can find you. If there is no chance of rain, you might want to place your signs the night before, but be prepared for "early birds" ringing your door bell at 6 a.m. and wanting a quick preview if you do.

caution Be careful about where you post your signs, especially on city property such as light poles and speed limit signs. I know that lots of people do it, but it is illegal and I would advise against it unless you get permission. Not only are your signs subject to removal, but you could be fined. Find out what the rules for posting signs are in your area when you inquire about whether you need a garage sale permit. Be mindful about posting your signs in other people's yards as well, unless you ask for permission.

Think through how a person will make their way to your house and find your sale. You can start by placing signs at a main thoroughfare and work toward your house, or the other way around. If there are two ways to get to your house from a main thoroughfare, you will need signage for both. Be sure you have made enough signs to direct people to your home, because you have gone through far too much work to make the mistake of people not being able to find you.

Merchandising Your Sale

Taking the extra time to logically display what you are selling will not only make it easier for shoppers to find what they are looking for, but will also result in your sale being more profitable. Try to get as many tables as you can to display your wares. People will spend more time looking at what you have if they don't have to bend down. Figure 14.3 has two good examples of how much better things will look (and how much more quickly they're likely to sell) when merchandised properly.

note Be sure to remove the signs when your sale is over and you have closed up. Nothing is more maddening than to make your way to someone's sale only to find it closed or to see a sign still hanging weeks after someone's sale is over.

FIGURE 14.3
These dishes and Xmas decorations will sell more easily and fetch a higher price fully displayed on a table rather than being stuck in a box.

If you don't have enough tables of your own, borrow some from friends and family or consider renting some, depending on how many small items you have for sale. You can create a makeshift table by laying a piece of plywood across two saw horses, two large boxes, or two picnic benches, as shown in Figure 14.4. Group like things together and put as many small items as you can on tables the night before. In the morning, simply open the garage door, carry the tables out on the driveway, and you are ready for business. Old bookcases and shelving units, such as those shown in Figure 14.5, can be used to display a wide variety of things.

FIGURE 14.4
This makeshift table makes a great display so people don't have to bend down to look at the merchandise.

FIGURE 14.5
These metal shelving units make it easy to showcase all kinds of bargains.

Here are some other great ideas that will help your stuff sell:

- Place large, attention-grabbing items out on the driveway or closer to the street where they are most visible. These are the things that will make it irresistible for the "drive by" shoppers to want to stop and check the rest of your stuff out.
- Clothing will sell much better hung up, as shown in Figure 14.6. If you don't have portable racks, try stringing some heavy-duty cord between two trees. Don't forget to check all the pockets for money and other personal items.

FIGURE 14.6
You will sell more clothing and receive a higher price for it if you hang it up.

- Get items as clean as you can by wiping them off or washing them, if appropriate. This will make them look newer and will help to bring a higher price.

- Place items with small pieces and parts in clear Ziploc® bags to keep them all together and write the price right on the bag.

- Some people love to dig through stuff in boxes and tubs and discover forgotten "treasures," so consider having a 25-cent and 50-cent box with all kinds of odds and ends.

- Have an extension cord plugged in and ready to demonstrate that electrical appliances and lamps really work.

If you have items in the garage that are not for sale, do yourself a favor and cover these things with old sheets, drop cloths, or moving blankets and rope these areas off to prevent people from going through your stuff.

To do list

- ❏ Recruit helpers.
- ❏ Set up a bank and cashier station.
- ❏ Remove large bills from the cashbox from time to time.
- ❏ Have fun.

Managing the Sale

If you follow the preparation advice in this chapter, you are destined to have a very profitable sale. However, here are some other things you will want to consider to ensure that your sale goes smoothly:

- Make sure you have plenty of help. With any luck at all, the first few hours of your sale are going to bring an onslaught of ready buyers; don't even think about trying to handle this by yourself. Not only is it unwise, it isn't safe either. At the very least, you will need a person dedicated to cashier duties and another to help you answer questions and watch the crowd. You will also need help in carrying the larger, attention-grabbing items and some of your tables stacked with stuff out onto the driveway.

- Do not open the garage door before you are ready, and make no exceptions. Serious shoppers often arrive early and, with any luck, will form a line down the driveway. You will be surprised at the tenacity and determination of people who will insist that they need for you to make an exception and let them in early. Resist the temptation, no matter how many times they ring the doorbell or how hard they knock on your door. You have advertised or posted your hours and they will just have to wait until the garage door goes up. You will be far too busy with last-minute details to worry about one person who might not wait for you to open.

- Do not allow people in your home for any reason unless you have items for sale in there as well. If so, do not allow them to roam through your entire house. Gather and confine items for sale to the rooms closest to the garage and restrict access to the rest of the house. Make sure that someone is in the house at all times. If there are just a few items for sale in the house, try to bring them outside or have large pictures of them on a sign in the garage with a price. Then if someone is really interested, you can escort them inside to see the items.

- Keep more expensive items near the cashier or in the garage—not on a table in the driveway or on the lawn—so you can watch them more closely.

> **caution** Don't serve or sell food or drinks that you make yourself. It can be against the law and if someone gets sick, they can sue you. It's not worth it.

Things You'll Need

- ❑ Helpers
- ❑ Cashbox
- ❑ Calculator
- ❑ Notebook and pen to record items sold
- ❑ Plastic and paper bags

Setting Up a Checkout Station

If you have friends or family members helping you with the sale, designate a competent person to be the cashier. This will alleviate any confusion over whether someone has paid or not. The larger the sale, the more important this job is.

Having a cashier is especially important in a multifamily sale because this person will record the sales for each family in a ledger that can be tallied at the end of the day, making it easier to divide the money. If this is going to be a smaller one-family sale, you might be able to get by with one or two people wearing aprons with pockets, but a single cashier is always preferable. Of course, if someone is in a hurry to buy an item and leave, you can take the money and alert the cashier that this person has paid to avoid an embarrassing situation when they leave. Don't forget to give the cashier the money when you get a free moment so that it can be properly accounted for.

> **tip** Start saving plastic and brown paper bags and boxes from the grocery store weeks in advance to bag people's purchases. Have plenty of newspaper on hand to wrap fragile items.

Set up a bank for the cashier in advance. Use a cashbox—one with dividers for coin and currency is preferable. Be sure to start off with one roll each of nickels, dimes, and quarters, 50 one-dollar bills and 50 dollars worth of five and ten dollar bills as well. You certainly don't want to lose a buyer because you couldn't change a large bill first thing in the morning, do you? You will also need a battery-operated or solar powered calculator to add up purchases.

> **tip** 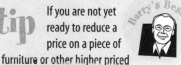 If you are not yet ready to reduce a price on a piece of furniture or other higher priced items, keep a notebook with the names and telephone numbers of people who have expressed interest in them and the price they are willing to pay. You will be so glad you did this when the sale is over and you still have these items left. Sometimes, people will offer you a lump sum to buy the remains of what you don't sell. You will want to write down their contact information as well.

Situate the cashier near the exit away from the garage, so they can easily see people come and go and stop someone if they appear to be walking away with something without paying for it. If an item has been marked down, be sure the seller has indicated that on the price tag to avoid embarrassment at checkout.

caution Be sure to continually take large denominations of bills out of the cashbox throughout the morning and put them in your pocket or in the house. Under no circumstances should you take checks from anyone you don't know or leave the cashbox unattended.

If people come in with large bags and backpacks or are purchasing your luggage, purses, and tote bags, the cashier should remember to look inside to be sure that they have not been stuffed full of other items. I'm sorry to have to even mention this, but sometimes people will conveniently forget to tell you.

Summary

You have learned all the essential elements of planning a successful garage or yard sale, including when to schedule it, how to price your items, and how to advertise and merchandise your sale. By following the advice in this chapter, you are sure to be well on your way to turning your castoffs into dollars and having some fun at the same time.

Hopefully when your sale is over, you will have sold just about everything, made more than you had expected, and be ready to give the rest away. If you aren't sure where to donate what remains, see Chapter 13 for some great ideas. On the other hand, if you had so much fun with this sale that you are hooked and convinced you would like to have another (and you have enough stuff left to make it worth your while), box it all up and label the boxes "Garage Sale." Then, when you or your neighbor decides to have another sale, you'll be well on your way to more fun and profit. Whatever you do, don't take the stuff back into your house under any circumstances, okay?

Part IV

Appendix

Resources and References

Product and Vendor Resources

The following sections provide information on the products mentioned in this book, as well as where to buy them.

Product Manufacturers and Vendors

Floor Products

Better Life Technology	www.BLTLLC.com
Fast-Flor	www.HomeOrganizers.ca
Premier Garage®	www.PremierGarage.com

Grid Systems

Elfa®	www.TheContainerStore.com
Garage Grids®	www.GarageGrids.com
Schulte®	www.SchulteStorage.com
	www.OrganizedLiving.com

Label Makers

Brother	www.Brother.com
Casio	www.Casio.com
Dymo	www.Dymo.com

Loft Storage

Hy-Loft®	www.HyLoft.com
Loft-It® Storage Lift System	www.Loft-It.com

Pegboard Systems and Accessories

Bunjipegs™	www.Bunjipeg.com
StorageTrack	www.HomeOrganizers.ca

Portable Storage Units

At Your Door Self Stor!	www.AtYourDoor.com
Door to Door Storage	www.DoorToDoorStorage.com
PODS (Portable On Demand Storage)	www.Pods.com

Sheds

Arrow	www.ArrowSheds.com
Rubbermaid®	www.Rubbermaid.com
Spirit Elements	www.SpiritElements.com

Sports Racks

ProStor	www.RacorInc.com
Rack Warehouse	www.RackWarehouse.com
Racor®	www.RacorInc.com

Storage: Cabinet and Wall-Mount Systems

ClosetMaid®	www.ClosetMaid.com
Coleman®	www.ColemanStorage.com
Crown Wall	www.HomeOrganizers.ca
Elfa®	www.TheContainerStore.com
Eurotec™	www.4garage.com
GarageTek®	www.GarageTek.com
Garage Grids®	www.GarageGrids.com
Gladiator™	www.GladiatorGW.com
A Place for Everything	www.APlaceForEverything.net
Premier Garage®	www.PremierGarage.com
Rubbermaid®	www.Rubbermaid.com
Schulte®	www.SchulteStorage.com
	www.OrganizedLiving.com
Slide-Lok	www.Slide-Lok.com
Space Logic™	www.CaseDirect.com/SpaceLogic.asp
StorageTrack	www.HomeOrganizers.ca
StoreWALL™	www.StoreWall.com

Tool Holders

Casabella	www.Casabella.com
Organize-Everything.com	www.Organize-Everything.com

Workbenches

ClosetMaid®	www.ClosetMaid.com
Coleman®	www.ColemanStorage.com
Sauder®	www.Sauder.com
	www.HotRodBySauder.com
Schulte®	www.SchulteStorage.com
	www.OrganizedLiving.com
StoreWALL™	www.StoreWall.com

Organizing Retailers

In-store—Locations Nationwide

The Container Store	www.TheContainerStore.com
Organized Living	www.OrganizedLiving.com

Online—Internet Shopping

www.OnLineOrganizing.com

www.Organize-Everything.com

www.StacksandStacks.com

Organizing Software

ARRANGE™	www.Smead.com
ItsDeductible®	www.ItsDeductible.com
The Paper Tiger®	www.ThePaperTiger.com
Arranging It All®	www.ArrangingItAll.com

Additional Resources

The following sections provide resources for finding a professional organizer in your area to help you achieve your organizing goals. These sections also provide further reading references and information on the options available for getting rid of the items you no longer need or want.

Books and Magazines

Allen, Sam. *Making Workbenches: Planning, Building, Outfitting.* Sterling Publishing Company, Inc., 1995.

American Garage. www.AmericanGarageMagazine.com. This magazine is scheduled to appear soon.

Berg, Phil. *Ultimate Garages.* Motorbooks International, 2003.

Brown, Connie. *Great Garages, Sheds & Outdoor Buildings: 145 Products You Can Build.* Home Planners LLC, 2001.

Obolensky, Kira. *Garage: Reinventing the Place We Park.* The Taunton Press, 2001.

Schleining, Lon. *The Workbench: A Complete Guide to Creating Your Perfect Workbench.* The Taunton Press, 2004.

West, Bill. *Your Garagenous Zone: Innovative Ideas for the Garage.* Paragon Garage Company, Ltd., 2004.

Professional Organizing Services

If you would like the help of a professional organizer to assist in organizing your garage, home, or business, here is a list of professional organizing associations that can help you find one.

National Association of Professional Organizers (NAPO) www.NAPO.net

Founded in 1985, NAPO is the Organizing Authority, with more than 3,200 members throughout the United States, Canada, and other countries around the world. The NAPO website features a free, automated referral system that enables you to find a professional organizer in your geographic area who is right for you.

National Study Group on Chronic Disorganization (NSGCD) www.NSGCD.org

NSGCD provides education on chronic disorganization and referrals to professional organizers who specialize in helping chronically disorganized clients and those with additional needs due to physical and mental disabilities.

Professional Organizers in Canada (POC) www.OrganizersInCanada.com

Founded in 2001, POC has more than 300 members working in the Canadian provinces. The POC website features a free, automated referral system that enables you to find a professional organizer in your geographic area who is right for you.

Outlets for Getting Rid of Items

Charitable Organizations

The Arc	www.TheArc.org
Bethesda	www.BLHS.org
Goodwill Industries	www.Goodwill.org
Habitat for Humanity	www.HabitatForHumanity.org
The Salvation Army	www.SalvationArmyUSA.org
Society of St. Vincent de Paul	www.SVDPUSA.org

Selling

Auction Drop	www.AuctionDrop.com
Craig's List	www.Craigsl ist.org
eBay	www.eBay.com

Hauling Service

1-800-GOT-JUNK?	www.1800GotJunk.com

Hazardous Waste

Earth 911	www.Earth911.org/master.asp
	www.CleanUp.org

Recycling

Battery recycling	www.BatteryRecycling.com
	www.RBRC.org
Freecycle	www.FreeCycle.org
Cell phones	www.WirelessFoundation.org
Clothing	www.DressForSuccess.org
	www.GlassSlipperProject.org
Computers	www.Dell.com
	www.Cristina.org
Eyeglasses	www.LensCrafters.com
Pet items	www.pets911.com
Steel	www.recycle-steel.org

Index